ASIA'S DYNAMIC LOCAL CHURCHES
SERVING DIALOGUE AND MISSION

Asia's Dynamic Local Churches

Serving Dialogue and Mission

James H. Kroeger, MM

Claretian
Communications

Jesuit
Communications

Asia's Dynamic Local Churches: Serving Dialogue and Mission
Copyright © 2014 by James H. Kroeger

Cover Photograph: Anthony V. Coloma
Illustrations: Jason K. Dy

Claretian Communications Foundation, Inc. is a pastoral endeavor of the Claretian Missionaries in the Philippines. Contact: Claretian Communications Foundation, Inc.; U.P.P.O. Box 4, Diliman; 1101 Quezon City, Philippines; Tel: 921-3984 / 922-9806; Fax: 921-6205; Email: cci@claret.org; www.claretianpublications.com

Jesuit Communications produces audio-visual and print media for evangelization and education. Contact: Jesuit Communications Foundation, Inc.; Sonolux Building, Ateneo de Manila University; Loyola Heights, Quezon City, Philippines; Tel: 426-5971 to 72; Fax: 426-5970; jcf@admu.edu.ph; www.ignaciana.org/jescom

---

Library of Congress Cataloging-in-Publication Data

Kroeger, James H.
    Asia's Dynamic Local Churches
    Serving Dialogue and Mission
        p. xii + 196 cm. 14.6 x 22.2
        ISBN: 978-621-8009-09-7

    1. Catholic Church—Asia. 2. Federation of Asian Bishops' Conferences. 3. Asia—Evangelization.
    4. Vatican Council (2nd : 1962-1965).
    I. Title. II. Kroeger, James H.

    BX1615 K75 2014
    282.5—dc21

CONTENTS

Foreword   vii

Introduction   ix

1. WAVES OF RENEWAL IN MISSION THEOLOGY
   Insights in the Vatican II Era   1

2. ASIA'S CHURCHES, THEOLOGY AND MISSION
   Four Decades of FABC Growth and Service   31

3. THE FAITH-CULTURE DIALOGUE IN ASIA
   Ten FABC Insights on Inculturation   53

4. WALKING THE PATH OF DIALOGUE IN ASIA
   FABC Wisdom on Interreligious Dialogue   79

5. TO LIVE IS TO EVANGELIZE
   Recent Popes and Integral Evangelization   109

6. BECOMING MISSIONARY LOCAL CHURCHES
   FABC Perspectives and Insights   137

7. NEW EVANGELIZATION TODAY
   Key Themes and Asian Links   169

Biographical Data   191

Books by James H. Kroeger   193

FOREWORD

The presentation of the Bishop Jonas Thaliath CMI Endowment Lectures of the Faculty of Theology at the Pontifical Athenaeum of Philosophy, Theology and Canon Law in Dharmaram Vidya Kshetram (DVK) in Bangalore, India, is an annual event. These lectures, year after year, provide theological enlightenment, pastoral guidance and socio-cultural dialogical engagement for the sons and daughters of the Church, especially the students and research scholars of DVK. In 2013-14 the lectures were delivered by James H. Kroeger, MM, under the theme: *Asia's Dynamic Local Churches*. His lectures, now available in print for a far wider audience of readers, are a great source of enlightenment. In this volume Kroeger presents Asian ecclesiological insights, practical guidelines, and needed pastoral engagements, with clear down-to-earth theological reflection.

Asia is the cradle of several major world religions. In the context of Asian vitality, which is embedded in the Asian plurality of peoples, cultures and religions, the Church has a vital role to play. The ecclesiology of Asia has grown through many centuries. An Asian ecclesiology does not basically play on the thrust of "conquest" as may have happened elsewhere. Rather, Asia stands on the organic progression in process enlightened by the Christian vision of salvation, as highlighted in *Ecclesia in Asia*, where Saint John Paul II states:

> It was in fact in Asia that God revealed and fulfilled his saving purpose from the beginning. He guided the patriarchs (Gen 12) and called Moses to lead his people to freedom (Ex 3:10). He spoke to his chosen people through many prophets, judges, kings and valiant women of faith. In "the fullness of time" (Gal 4:4), he sent his only-begotten Son, Jesus Christ the Savior, who took flesh as an Asian! (*Ecclesia in Asia* 1).

As the Savior was historically born an Asian, the Church in Asia also has to be born as Asian. The birth pangs "to be born as Asian" are ever challenging and fruitful for the Asian Church. This quest has received much impetus from the inspiration and teachings of the Second Vatican Council. The individual local Churches in Asia have manifested their identity and individuality in seeking to attain a "new way of being Church in Asia." This "becoming" and "being" modes of the Church in Asia have been enhanced by the dynamic services and leadership of the Federation of Asian Bishops' Conferences (FABC).

Four decades of FABC reflection (1972-2012) has maturely recognized and developed the needed dialogue with Asia's peoples, cultures and religions. The "reign of God" is a wider universal reality than the Church. In Asia, the Church has to be ever alert to recognize how that "reign of God" is realized within and outside the Church in many sectors of Asia's peoples, cultures and religions. Dialogue is the mode, means and first fruits of evangelization and salvation in the Asian context of plurality and diversity. In such a context, the "universality of the Spirit" by which the economy of salvation progresses becomes clearer. Evangelizing culture and inculturating faith are key steps to be taken in Asia. This process, as Kroeger would put it, focuses on "bringing the light and power of the Gospel into the multi-religious and pluri-cultural reality of contemporary Asia" (*see*: Chapter 4, page 79).

The thrust of integral evangelization, based on *Evangelii Nuntiandi* and *Redemptoris Missio*, as reflected in *Ecclesia in Asia*, is spelled out on the basis of the theological synthesis of the FABC vision in this volume. In the final chapter, the ten defining traits of "new evangelization" remind every segment of the Church and every Christian of the need of evangelizing with Christian joy and hope in the modern world.

Dr. Thomas Kollamparampil CMI
Member: International Theological Commission
Dean: Faculty of Theology,
DVK, Bangalore, India.

INTRODUCTION

The phenomenal and dynamic growth of the Asian Churches in the fifty-year Vatican II era has graciously been blessed by God's providence. The renewing and creative Spirit of God continues to engender life in Asia's peoples, cultures and religions, her history, traditions and arts, her struggle for true and authentic life. There has been a marvelous expansion, yes in numbers, but more significantly in depth of understanding and reflection. Led by the Spirit, the local Churches of Asia have more deeply perceived their self-identity and their call to mission, looking interiorly (*ad intra*) and exteriorly (*ad extra*), committed to genuine love and service of all the peoples of Asia. By God's grace, to employ an expression of the Federation of Asian Bishops' Conferences (FABC), the past many decades following in the wake of Vatican II, have witnessed "*a new way of being Church in Asia.*"

Significant impetus for the renewal of the Church in Asia emerged from the Second Vatican Council as well as from the November 1970 visit of Pope Paul VI to the Asian continent. One may identify an impressive series of initiatives that have fostered a renewed vision and praxis of a genuinely inculturated Asian Church. Consider the following Spirit-inspired movements, constituting an Asian vision of a renewed Church. As noted by various FABC assemblies, there has been: • a movement towards "a Church of the Poor and a Church of the Young"; • a movement toward a "truly local Church, incarnate in a people"; • a movement toward "deep interiority" and becoming a "deeply praying community"; • a movement toward "an authentic community of faith"; • a movement toward "active integral evangelization, toward a new sense of mission"; • a movement toward "empowerment of men and women"; • a movement toward "active involvement in generating and serving life"; • a movement toward "the triple

dialogue with other faiths, with the poor and with the cultures";
• a movement toward a "participatory Church" and a
"communion of communities"; • a movement toward existence
"in solidarity with the whole of creation."

This publication emerges from an intense interest in and
serious study of the "Asian Church" over several decades. It is
presented in seven thematic chapters that reflect a 2013 lecture
series at Dharmaram Vidya Kshetram in Bangalore, India. The
book seeks to capture and highlight the central and pivotal
theological-missiological themes emerging in the Asian Church
in recent decades, themes which reflect the Spirit-inspired
movements already noted earlier. Pope Benedict XVI asserted
(September 20, 2012) that "the new evangelization started
precisely with the Council, which Blessed John XXIII saw as a
new Pentecost." Likewise, the profound and extensive renewal
in and of the Church in Asia is intimately linked with "living
the Council in Asia."

Chapter One is devoted to exploring nine "waves of renewal
in mission theology" in the light of the insights of the Second
Vatican Council. The image of a "wave" is helpful to appreciate
the various movements that have arrived and continue to
arrive on the shores of Asia's local Churches. This first chapter
identifies the waves (e.g. inculturation, dialogue, etc.); some
subsequent chapters treat the same themes more extensively,
linking them into the Asian context, frequently employing the
theological materials of the FABC and *Ecclesia in Asia*.

Chapter Two is an overview of the most recent FABC plenary
assembly, held in December 2012 in Vietnam, bearing the
theme: "FABC at Forty Years—Responding to the Challenges of
Asia: New Evangelization." The piece includes a presentation
of the pivotal characteristics and emphases of four decades of
FABC theology. In addition, the inspiring text of the "Message
of Tenth FABC Plenary Assembly" is found in an appendix. As
one reads and absorbs these materials, one becomes convinced
of the dynamic presence of God's Spirit at work in the local
Churches of Asia.

The next chapter takes up in great detail the question of the "faith-culture dialogue" in the Asian context. In its four decades of existence, the FABC has given significant thought as to how "inculturation" is to be best achieved in and through the local Churches in this continent. In ten distinct points, the primary focuses of the "rooting of the faith" in Asia are explored. The question is a crucial and challenging one, because it has been noted by the FABC that "if the Asian Churches do not discover their own identity, they will have no future."

Chapter Four addresses the topic of interfaith dialogue in the Asian context, employing the helpful insights of the FABC corpus of wisdom and experience. Once again, this is an area that calls for insightful theological reflection and committed pastoral action. One need only consider the fact that 85% of all the world's non-Christians live in Asia, where less than 3% of the total population is Christian. Repeatedly, the Asian bishops have asserted that *dialogue* (properly understood) is the *mode of mission* most fitted to the Asian reality.

The fifth chapter explores the rich concept of integral evangelization. The thought of two popes on this matter is presented, using Paul VI's *Evangelii Nuntiandi* and John Paul II's *Redemptoris Missio*. In a final synthesis section, the five "principal elements" of integral evangelization are identified, citing passages from Paul VI, John Paul II, and *Ecclesia in Asia*, adding brief references to the beautiful *Evangelii Gaudium* of Pope Francis.

Chapter Six presents a pivotal topic in the theological synthesis of FABC theology: the identity and role of the *local Church*. The experience and thought of the Asian Churches is profound, certainly some of the best insights on a vision of local Church—anywhere in the world. Here one also finds a presentation of the Asian "Pastoral Spiral" theological method, as well as a brief overview of some "Asian-born" mission initiatives in the Vatican II era.

The final chapter explores the current topic of "new

evangelization." An effort is made to link this initiative into the realities and challenges of Asia. It is striking to note that so many of the key themes needing to be addressed in the "new evangelization" already appear in the documents of Vatican II. To be a contemporary and effective "new evangelizer" demands a rediscovery of the profound insights of the Second Vatican Council!

Readers will notice some similar matter appearing in a few places; this became inevitable, since the author designed *each chapter* to be an *integral presentation*, capable of being read independently of the other chapters. In addition, some few themes have appeared in other published writings of the author, who is grateful for the generous indulgence of the publications.

Finally, the author expresses his gratitude to the CMI community at the Pontifical Athenaeum of Dharmaram Vidya Kshetram for the opportunity to be a "visiting professor" and present these materials, which may be termed "an ecclesiology of the Asian Churches," appropriate to the contemporary challenges of the "new evangelization"! It is the author's fervent wish and prayer that these materials will promote a renewed commitment to evangelization by dedicated "missionary disciples" (EG 120) who are themselves "joyful evangelizers" since they have discovered the profound joy of Christ and his Gospel.

James H. Kroeger, MM
Pentecost 2014

WAVES OF RENEWAL IN MISSION THEOLOGY
Insights in the Vatican II Era

In the Asian context in particular, the theology and praxis of mission and evangelization have experienced a genuine renewal in the fifty years since the opening of the Second Vatican Council. Saint John XXIII summoned the Council on January 25, 1959; the first session was on October 11, 1962. The Church joyfully celebrated the golden anniversary in 2012 of this milestone, the most significant religious event of the last century.

Recalling this pivotal five-decade milestone (1962-2012), the Church can profitably ask: How has the Catholic Church—especially in Asia—*received* Vatican II? Used as a theological category today, "reception" describes that process whereby the Christian community acknowledges, accepts, and integrates the insights of a Church event, teaching, or experience (e.g. a Council, a Synod, an encyclical or pastoral letter). One necessarily asks: have Catholics in general, and missionaries and religious in particular, "owned" or personally appropriated the Council's vision of the Church and her mission? Have attitudes, beliefs, and behaviors been transformed and renewed? What are some future challenges? Probably, the full reception of Vatican II is only just beginning!

The Spirit-inspired renewal envisioned by Vatican II has come in what this author identifies as "waves." There may be small and large waves, gentle as well as forceful ones. Waves often come slowly, as if we hardly notice. However, we see their effects on the shore, moving the sand, eroding the earth in one place and depositing it in another. We know the constant, continuous action of waves; one has hardly reached shore and another is approaching after it. The image of the "wave" may prove helpful for us to appreciate what has happened and continues to unfold in the Church. This presentation examines the waves of renewal in the Church's theological understanding of her mission of evangelization. Nine specific areas (waves of mission renewal) will be examined briefly—and linked into the Asian context.

I. An Integral View of Evangelization. In his message for World Mission Day in October 2011, Pope Benedict XVI noted that the Church has the urgent duty to proclaim the Gospel. The pope continued: "This task has not lost its urgency. On the contrary, 'the mission of Christ Redeemer, entrusted to the Church, is still far from being accomplished.... We must commit ourselves with all our energies in its service (RM 1)'." The pope stated clearly the scope of the mission of evangelization: "The universal mission involves all, everywhere, and always."

For many Catholics the term evangelization is a generally unfamiliar and relatively new concept; only recently has it been gaining wider currency. Thanks to the Second Vatican Council as well as recent popes, evangelization is now located at the center of the Church's identity and mission—at least theoretically and theologically. Recent discussions have contributed to an understanding of evangelization in all its rich, complex, multi-faceted, and interrelated dimensions; thus, contemporary evangelization is necessarily viewed holistically and integrally.

Vatican II speaks of evangelization in a variety of contexts: it is especially the bishops' task to promote evangelization by the faithful (CD 6); it is associated with the mission of the laity (AA 2, 6, 20, 26; LG 35); priests are to learn the methods of evangelization (PO 19); the Eucharist is the source and summit of all evangelization (PO 5). The Decree on Missions (AG) is replete with references: "the specific purpose of missionary activity is evangelization and the planting of the Church" (6); "the Church has the obligation and the sacred right to evangelize" (7); catechists have an important task to evangelize (17), as do the laity (21); the call to evangelize arises from a charism of the Spirit (23); various roles are fulfilled by missionary institutes (27), Propaganda Fidei (29), the People of God (35, 36), bishops and priests (38), religious institutes (40), and young Churches (LG 17).

Pope Paul VI (1963-1978) will always be remembered as a modern missionary pope; he made missionary journeys to all continents; he authored *Evangelii Nuntiandi* (EN), which became the *magna carta* for Catholic evangelization in the last quarter of the second millennium of Christianity. Without doubt, EN is one of the most important ecclesial documents of the post-Vatican II era. It presents a concise, inspiring, and programmatic challenge for the Church to enthusiastically engage in her God-given mission to preach the Gospel to the contemporary world—to living peoples, with their aspirations and anxieties, their cultures and religions, their hopes and conflicts. Although Paul VI did not specifically use the term "new evangelization," his writings, especially *Evangelii Nuntiandi*, boldly address the topic of evangelization in the modern world.

Karol Jósef Wojtyla was elected pope on October 16, 1978 and took the name John Paul II. Under his leadership the papal ministry became focused on evangelization and global mission; he traveled to numerous countries, strengthened local Christian communities, encountered followers of other religions, spoke on the social teachings of the Church, canonized saints and honored blesseds, and met with youth and government leaders. Pope John Paul II asserted that the Second Vatican Council set the direction for his papacy. His eighth encyclical *Redemptoris Missio* (RM) was issued on December 7, 1990; it celebrates the twenty-fifth anniversary of Vatican II's Mission Decree *Ad Gentes* and the fifteenth anniversary of Paul VI's *Evangelii Nuntiandi*. In RM, the pope sounds a clarion call to all Church sectors to renew their enthusiasm and commitment to evangelize the world.

Today the Church sees that the "principal elements" of mission and evangelization are: **(a)** presence and witness of life;

(b) commitment to social development and human liberation;
(c) interreligious dialogue; **(d)** explicit Gospel proclamation
and catechesis; and, **(e)** prayer, contemplation, and liturgical
life. In a word, the one evangelizing mission of the Church
is comprised of several component elements and authentic
forms. This integral or holistic view has served the Church well
over the past decades. Viewing evangelization through five
of its principal elements results in clarity, insight, and proper
integration. This is a Catholic vision of evangelization. Allow
a brief word about each of these five elements.

For Paul VI, who sees that "evangelizing means bringing
the Good News into all strata of humanity" (EN 18), **Christian
presence and witness of life** form the "initial act of
evangelization" (EN 21). Daily activities, living in harmony,
lives as individuals of integrity, duties in the community—all
these are to be a basic "faith-witness" that demonstrates how
Christian living is shaped by Christian faith and values. Through
this wordless witness, "Christians stir up irresistible questions
in the hearts of those who see how they live" (EN 21). And, in
today's world, people desire and respect authentic witnesses
(cf. EN 41; RM 11, 42; EA 42). Blessed Mother Teresa of Calcutta
(beatified on October 19, 2003), known for her loving and
selfless care of the poorest of the poor, is an "icon" of Christian
presence, life, and service (EA 7). In Asia, a "genuinely religious
person readily wins respect and following" (EA 23); Christian
life itself is a proclamation.

Community living as good neighbors based on faith
convictions should naturally issue in a **commitment to social
development and human liberation**, a genuine service of
humanity. This means serving the most unfortunate, witnessing
to justice, defending the integrity of creation. This dimension
of evangelization includes the whole area of social concerns,
ranging from peace-building, education and health services,
to promoting family life and good government. The area of
human development or human promotion is a vast area of
the Church's evangelizing mission (cf. EN 18-19, 29-33; RM
58-60; EA 32-41). In many parts of the world, the Church

has distinguished herself in education, health care, and social service (EA 7).

All evangelizing activities are inserted into specific contexts; particularly in Asia, these activities naturally assume an interreligious dimension. Thus, the Church in Asia, similar to most places in the world of today, accomplishes her mission in pluralistic and diverse cultures; she enters into **interreligious dialogue**, cooperating with the followers of the great religious traditions. Interreligious dialogue takes many forms; there are the dialogues of daily life, deeds of service, religious experts, and faith experience, as well as other forms. John Paul II asserts: "Interreligious dialogue is a part of the Church's evangelizing mission" (RM 55). This dialogue emerges from one's faith convictions. In contemporary circumstances, dialogue with religions and cultures is the truly appropriate Christian response (cf. EN 20, 53; RM 52-54, 55-57; EA 31; cf. 21-22). The Asian Bishops (FABC) have noted that dialogue is the mode of mission in the Asian context.

In mission today there is the role of **explicit Gospel proclamation and catechesis**. This dimension of evangelization includes preaching, catechesis on Christian life, teaching the content of the faith; in a word, this means "telling the Jesus story." When the Holy Spirit opens the door and when the time is opportune, Christians are not timid; they do tell the story of Jesus, giving explicit witness and testimony to the faith. Others are invited, in freedom of conscience, to follow, to come to know Jesus. Through proclamation Christians themselves are further instructed in their faith; this is the process through which the Christian faith is communicated to the next generation of believers (cf. EN 22, 27, 42; RM 44-51; EA 10-14).

Finally, the Church's mission of integral evangelization will necessarily include **prayer, contemplation and liturgical life**. No one can effectively be engaged in mission without a strong faith and prayer-life. Evangelization needs holy men and women who are themselves on fire with the love of

Christ; spreading the fire of the Gospel will be accomplished only by those already burning with an experience of Christ. Holiness is an irreplaceable condition for evangelizers. The "God-experience" achieved in prayer and contemplation, in sacramental and liturgical life, will illumine and transform all other dimensions of evangelization (cf. EN 23, 43-44, 47; RM 46-49, 87-92; EA 23-25).

Obviously, these five dimensions of an integral understanding of evangelization complement and reinforce each other. In speaking of the complexity of the Church's evangelizing action, Paul VI gave a timely admonition: "Any partial and fragmentary definition which attempts to render the reality of evangelization in all its richness, complexity and dynamism does so only at the risk of impoverishing it and even of distorting it." The pope continued: "It is impossible to grasp the concept of evangelization unless one tries to keep in view all its essential elements" (EN 17). The Church's mission is "one and indivisible, having one origin and one final purpose; but within it there are different responsibilities and different kinds of activities" (EA 42).

II. Universal Availability of Salvation. Although the universal availability of salvation has been held by the Church in one way or another since the days of Saint Ambrose in the fourth century, Vatican II gave the Church a breakthrough. In *Lumen Gentium* 16 the Council asserted that salvation is available to Jews, Muslims, those who seek the "unknown God," and even to those who have no faith in God at all. Indeed, God "wants everyone to be saved and reach full knowledge of the truth" (I Tim. 2:4).

The pivotal word here is *available*; God does not deny anyone salvation if they follow their conscience and strive to lead a good life (they are already being moved by God's grace). In a word, salvation is *available but not automatic*. Human response and cooperation with God are necessary factors in the reception of God's free gift of salvation. God is not stingy with his grace! In addition, one must *not* conclude that all religions are equal or that there is no urgency to continue proclaiming the Good News. Vatican II asserts that Catholics "ought to believe that the Holy Spirit in a manner known to God offers everyone the possibility of being associated with this paschal mystery" (GS 22). Pope John Paul II has made frequent use of this quote, citing it three times in *Redemptoris Missio* (6, 10, 28). In this context, one must ask the related question: "If the grace of God is universally available, what then is our *motivation* for mission?" [See *Appendix A* for an expression of mission motivation as enunciated by the Asian Bishops (FABC)].

As a corollary to appreciating the universal availability of salvation, one needs to reflect on the role of the Holy Spirit in God's design of salvation. Vatican II and its program of *aggiornamento* bring to the fore the role of the Holy Spirit in the Church, a dimension underemphasized in many earlier presentations of mission. *Ad Gentes*, the Council's Decree on the Church's Missionary Activity, pointed out that the Spirit unceasingly accompanies and guides the Church in her apostolic activities. The Spirit "furnishes the Church with various gifts, both hierarchical and charismatic. He vivifies ecclesiastical institutions as a kind of soul and instills into the hearts of the faithful the same mission spirit which motivated Christ himself" (AG 4). This same Spirit often anticipates the evangelizer's action, opening people's hearts to the Gospel message.

Pope Paul VI is eloquent when presenting the role of the Holy Spirit in missionary activity. "Evangelization will never be possible without the action of the Holy Spirit.... In fact, it is only after the coming of the Holy Spirit on the day of Pentecost that the Apostles depart to all the ends of the earth in order to begin the great work of the Church's evangelization.... Techniques of evangelization are good, but even the most advanced ones could not replace the gentle action of the Spirit.... It must be said that the Holy Spirit is the principal agent of evangelization.... Through the Holy Spirit the Gospel penetrates to the heart of the world" (EN 75).

John Paul II devotes an entire chapter in *Redemptoris Missio* (21-30) to the pivotal role of the Spirit in evangelization. All mission is "a sending forth in the Spirit" (22). The Spirit gives assurance that evangelizers "will not be alone in this task" (23). From the Spirit the apostle receives "the ability to bear witness to Jesus with 'boldness'" (24). "The Spirit's presence and activity affect not only individuals, but also society and history, peoples, cultures and religions" (28). "Whatever the Spirit brings about in human hearts and in the history of peoples, in cultures and religions, serves as a preparation for the Gospel" (29). Again, John Paul II reiterates that the Spirit is "the principal agent of mission" (30).

In the multi-cultural and pluri-religious Asian context, the action of the Spirit is paramount. "The Spirit gathers into unity all kinds of people, with their different customs, resources, and talents, making the Church a sign of the communion of all humanity.... [Thus] the Holy Spirit is the prime agent of evangelization" (EA 17). The Church looks to the Holy Spirit to continue to prepare the peoples of Asia for the saving dialogue with the Savior of all.... Committed to being a genuine sign and instrument of the Spirit's action in the complex realities of Asia..., the Church ceaselessly cries out: Come, Holy Spirit! Fill the hearts of your faithful and enkindle in them the fire of your love" (*Ecclesia in Asia* 18).

III. Church's Missionary Nature. Vatican II forcefully declared: "The pilgrim Church is missionary by her very nature. For it is from the mission of the Son and the mission of the Holy Spirit that she takes her origin, in accordance with the decree of God the Father" (AG 2). Christians believe in a Trinitarian God, who is not just the founder of a missionary community, the Church, but a God who is inherently missionary. The *missio Dei* was already operative before the Church came into existence. This theology locates mission at the very center of what the Church is and what she is called to be and to do.

Pope Paul VI asserts that missionary evangelization is the "vocation proper to the Church." He continues: "We wish to confirm once more that the task of evangelizing all people constitutes the essential mission of the Church." Evangelizing lies at "her deepest identity." She "exists in order to evangelize." She "is linked to evangelization in her most intimate being" (EN 14-15). The emphasis is clear: the Church is mission; she does not only do some activities that foster mission. The theologian Emil Brunner captured the Church's missionary identity well: "The Church exists by mission as fire exists by burning."

This missionary identity of the Church is primarily lived out and actualized through the local Churches. At the time of Vatican II, ecclesiology had a clear universalist emphasis; the Council facilitated a renewed awakening of the importance of the local Church. This has resulted in a richer understanding of the full missionary responsibility of the local Christian community. Vatican II asserted that the Church of Christ is fully present "in all legitimate local congregations" (LG 26); thus, as the Roman document *Dialogue and Mission* (14) asserts: "Every local church is responsible for the totality of mission."

Probably some of the best pastoral-mission theology on the local Church is to be found in the documents of the Federation of Asian Bishops' Conferences (FABC). The Asian bishops assert: "The primary focus of our task of evangelization then, at this time in our history, is the building up of a truly local Church" (FABC I: 9). "For the Asian Churches, the decisive new phenomenon ... will be the emergence of genuine Christian communities in Asia—Asian in their way of thinking, praying, living, communicating their own Christ-experience to others.... If the Asian Churches do not discover their own identity, they will have no future" (ACMC 14). Asia's bishops have consistently promoted a "new way of being Church" and that "the acting subject of mission is the *local Church* living and acting in communion with the universal Church" (FABC V: 8.0; 3.3.1). In all of this, FABC and its vision of Church become "Asia's continuing Vatican II."

It is valid to assert that the actualization of the renewed vision of the Church from the Council finds its first realization or actualization in the local Church. An example of this would be the effort to live Christianity ecumenically (though living interreligiously would have a greater urgency in Asia). In its document on ecumenism, Vatican II called upon all Christians to bear witness to their common hope (UR 12). The Council also noted that the divisions among Christians are a serious hindrance to the preaching of the Gospel and an authentic witness of life (UR 1).

Paul VI wrote of the importance of the search for Christian unity; he sought to emphasize "the sign of unity among Christians as the way and instrument of evangelization" (EN 77). In his encyclical *Ut Unum Sint*, John Paul II noted that it is impossible to authentically proclaim the Gospel which speaks of reconciliation, if at the same time, one is not concerned for reconciliation among Christians (UUS 98).

During the Asian Synod (1998), the Synod Fathers "acknowledged that 'the scandal of a divided Christianity is a great obstacle for evangelization in Asia.' In fact, the division among Christians is seen as a counter-witness to Jesus Christ by many in Asia who are searching for harmony and unity through their own religions and cultures" (EA 30). In Asia, "ecumenical dialogue and interreligious dialogue constitute a veritable vocation for the Church" (EA 29).

IV. Culture within the Evangelization Process. Today the imperative of inculturation is an accepted dimension of building up an authentic local Church. However, the use of the term first appeared only as recently as 1970 when Pope Paul VI met with 180 Asian bishops in Manila (cf. *Asian Bishops' Meeting* 24). "Inculturation" first appears in a papal document when John Paul II uses it (1985) in *Slavorum Apostoli* (18, 21, 27) and (1990) in *Redemptoris Missio* (52-54). Through inculturation the Church tries to reformulate and integrate Christian life and doctrine within the thought-patterns of each people.

Paul VI noted that: "what matters is to evangelize man's

culture and cultures (not in a purely decorative way as it were by applying a thin veneer, but in a vital way, in depth and right to their very roots)" (EN 20). This in-depth preaching of the Gospel has met difficulties in the past and will always face many challenges, due to the diversity, uniqueness, and fluidity of culture. The Council sets forth the challenge: "Faithful to her own tradition and at the same time conscious of her universal mission, [the Church] ... can enter into communion with various cultural modes, to her own enrichment and theirs too" (GS 58). This wave of mission renewal vigorously promotes evangelization deeply rooted in people's lives and values.

Related to an appreciation of culture, the evangelizing Church needs to be attentive to the "shapers" of culture. Today one may assert that a pivotal influence on culture is social communication. Vatican II in its document on the instruments of social communication, *Inter Mirifica*, notes: "The Catholic Church has been commissioned by the Lord Christ to bring salvation to everyone, and is consequently bound to proclaim the Gospel. Hence, she judges it part of her duty to preach the news of redemption with the aid of the instruments of social communication, and to instruct humanity as well in their worthy use" (IM 3).

With clarity, Paul VI noted the great influence of mass media on the world today. He writes: "Our century is characterized by the mass media or means of social communication, and the first proclamation, catechesis, or the further deepening of the faith cannot do without these means.... When they are put at the service of the Gospel, they are capable of increasing almost indefinitely the area in which the Word of God is heard.... In them she finds a modern and effective version of the pulpit" (EN 45).

In his mission encyclical John Paul II speaks at length about the "world of communication." He asserts: "Since the very evangelization of modern culture depends to a great extent on the influence of the media, it is not enough to use the media simply to spread the Christian message and the Church's authentic teaching. It is also necessary to integrate that message into the 'new culture' created by modern communications. This is a complex issue ... [and it involves] new ways of communicating, with new languages, new techniques, and a new psychology" (RM 37).

The comprehensive vision of evangelization put forth in *Ecclesia in Asia* observes: "Inevitably, the Church's evangelizing mission too is deeply affected by the impact of the mass media.... The exceptional role played by the means of social communication in shaping the world, its cultures and ways of thinking has led to rapid and far-reaching changes in Asian societies.... The Church needs to explore ways of thoroughly integrating the mass media into her pastoral planning and activity, so that by their effective use, the Gospel's power can reach out still further to individuals and entire peoples, and infuse Asian cultures with the values of the Kingdom" (EA 48).

V. Laity's Full Participation in the Church's Mission. One could assert that the Church's mission of evangelization is too important to be left to the clergy and religious alone; thus, in Vatican II one finds a renewed emphasis on the missionary nature of the *entire* Church. Every baptized member of the Church is equally an evangelizer, whether layperson, ordained, or religious. An integral vision of evangelization engages the entire Church (from top to bottom; especially, all the local Churches), all states of life (lay, religious, ordained, married, single), all apostolic activities and forms of witness (the five principal elements, noted earlier in section one).

It must be asserted that this emphasis on everyone's call to mission is not superficially based on the desire to have "more workers for the job." A profound and beautiful theology of Christian baptism and identity underlies this emphasis. *Christifideles Laici* (33) speaks of the laity's missionary responsibility: "The lay faithful, precisely because they are members of the Church, have the vocation and mission of proclaiming the Gospel; they are prepared for this work by the sacraments of Christian initiation and by the gifts of the

Holy Spirit." Laity are full-fledged evangelizers; mission is both their right and duty within the Church; they are not missionary due to some kind of "delegation of mission" coming from a priest or even a bishop. "By the grace and call of Baptism and Confirmation, all lay people are missionaries" (EA 45). This wave of renewal is still not fully recognized; it offers great potential for the Church.

Indeed, an older vision of mission and evangelization often saw that mission responsibility was the special concern of priests and sisters, apostolic associations, or various missionary orders of men and women. While these groups remain committed to their founding charism, the Second Vatican Council insisted that "the pilgrim Church is missionary by her very nature" (AG 2) and that "the work of evangelization is a basic duty of the People of God" and everyone must "do their share in missionary work among the nations" (AG 35). In a word, the Church is missionary "from top to bottom," involving everyone—bishops, priests, sisters, laity, and youth.

For Paul VI "it is the whole Church that receives the mission to evangelize, and the work of each individual member is important for the whole" (EN 15). The pope devoted one entire chapter of *Evangelii Nuntiandi* to the "Workers for Evangelization" (59-73). Thus, the commission to spread the Gospel is given to the universal Church (61), the local Churches (62), the pope (67), bishops and priests (68), religious (69), the laity (70), the family (71), and young people (72). One should find in the Church a variety of "diversified ministries" (73)—all at the service of missionary evangelization.

Similar to Paul VI's *Evangelii Nuntiandi*, one finds an entire chapter on "Leaders and Workers in the Missionary Apostolate" in John Paul II's *Redemptoris Missio* (61-76). Several of the same groups noted by Paul VI are mentioned by John Paul II; however, he devotes special sections to "life-long" *ad gentes* missionaries (65-66), diocesan priests (67), contemplatives (69), missionary religious sisters (70), catechists (73), episcopal conferences (76), and the Pontifical Mission Societies (84).

Thus, since "all Christians share responsibility for missionary activity," "missionary cooperation" becomes an imperative as diverse communities and individuals share and exercise their "right and duty" of evangelization (RM 77).

Ecclesia in Asia recognizes the multiple and diverse contributions of missionaries over the centuries. During the "Asian Synod" (1998) the Synod Fathers took advantage of the occasion "to express in a very special way their gratitude to all the missionaries, men and women, religious and lay, foreign and local, who brought the message of Jesus Christ and the gift of faith. A special word of gratitude again must be expressed to all the particular Churches which have sent and still send missionaries to Asia" (EA 20). In the same document, John Paul II noted that the challenge still remains; "I cannot fail to urge the Church in Asia to send forth missionaries, even though she herself needs laborers in the vineyard" (EA 44).

VI. Priesthood and Religious Life are Inherently Missionary. Vatican II and subsequent theological reflection emphasize the inherent organic bonding of priesthood and religious life with mission. The Council notes: "The spiritual gift which priests receive at their ordination prepares them not for any limited or narrow mission, but for the widest scope of the universal mission of salvation 'even to the very ends of the earth' (Acts 1:8). For every priestly ministry shares in the universality of the mission entrusted by Christ to his apostles" (PO 10).

Pope John Paul II has spoken frequently on the inherent missionary nature of the ordained priesthood. His mission encyclical states: "All priests must have the mind and heart of missionaries—open to the needs of the Church and the world, with concern for those farthest away…. Especially in those areas where Christians are a minority [Asia], priests must be filled with special missionary zeal and commitment" (RM 67). In *Pastores Dabo Vobis* (32) the pope writes: "In the exercise of their ministry and the witness of their lives, priests have the duty to form the community entrusted to them as a truly missionary community." The title that John Paul II gave to his message for World Mission Sunday in 1990 was: "Every Priest a Missionary."

Regarding religious life, the Second Vatican Council noted in *Perfectae Caritatis* [On the Renewal and Adaptation of Religious Life] (8): "There are in the Church very many communities, both clerical and lay, which devote themselves to various apostolic tasks.... In these communities apostolic and charitable activity belongs to the very nature of the religious life.... Therefore, the whole religious life of their members should be inspired by an apostolic spirit...." Renewal is needed here; many priests and religious continue to see themselves only in a pastoral role, rather than in a missionary role.

One pivotal dimension of the "missionary identity" of priests and religious is the need to be intensely interested in the profound corpus of the Church's social teaching. Vatican II affirmed that all Catholics (including Church leaders) must always be "attentive to the common good as related to the principles of the moral and social teaching of the Church" (AA 31). Christians are called to involve themselves in temporal affairs, so that "the social order and its development will unceasingly work to the benefit of the human person" (GS 26). The Church's social teaching and involvement spring from the profound realization that "God's Spirit, who with a marvelous providence directs the unfolding of time and renews the face of the earth, is present within these human developments" (GS 26).

Consistent with an integral vision of evangelization, Paul VI affirms that "the Church links human development and salvation in Jesus Christ, but she never identifies [equates] them" (EN 35). "The Church considers it to be undoubtedly important to build up structures which are more human, more just, more respectful of the rights of the person and less oppressive and less enslaving, but she is conscious that the best structures and the most idealized systems soon become inhuman if the inhuman inclinations of the human heart are not made wholesome" (EN 36). Thus, she continually promotes her moral and social teaching.

John Paul II consistently emphasizes Church social teaching and involvement. He notes that there are many places "where action on behalf of integral development and human liberation from all forms of oppression are most urgently needed" (RM 58). The pope affirms: "Authentic human development must be rooted in an ever deeper evangelization" (RM 58). As a force for liberation and development, the Church focuses on the human person, realizing that *"Man is the principal agent of development"* (RM 58).

Church reflection from the Asian context on social involvement is insightful. "The social doctrine of the Church, which proposes a set of principles for reflection, criteria for judgment and directives for action, is addressed in the first place to the members of the Church. It is essential that the faithful engaged in human promotion should have a firm grasp of this precious body of teaching and make it part of their evangelizing mission" (EA 32).

VII. Interreligious Dialogue, An Essential Element of Evangelization. One of the truly remarkable waves of mission renewal in the wake of Vatican II has been the Church's commitment to elucidating the vision and encouraging the practice of interfaith dialogue. It was only in 1964 in his first encyclical *Ecclesiam Suam* that Pope Paul VI introduced dialogue as a framework for envisioning the mission of the Church in the contemporary world.

The Second Vatican Council issued an entire document on the relationship of the Church with the followers of other faiths (*Nostra Aetate*). "The Catholic Church rejects nothing which is true and holy in these religions.... The Church therefore has this exhortation for her sons and daughters: prudently and lovingly, through dialogue and collaboration with the followers of other religions, and in witness of Christian faith and life, acknowledge, preserve, and promote the spiritual and moral goods found among these people, as well as the values in their society and culture" (NA 2).

Popes Paul VI and John Paul II find no essential conflict between proclamation and authentic interfaith dialogue. Perhaps his greatest affirmation of the importance of dialogue [already noted] is Pope Paul VI's first encyclical letter *Ecclesiam Suam* (1964) which is heavily devoted to dialogue as a pathway for the Church. One decade later in 1975, he reiterates the Church's profound respect for other religions, but notes that this respect does not imply that the Church would refrain from the proclamation of Jesus Christ (EN 53).

John Paul II devotes three full sections (55-57) of *Redemptoris Missio* to exploring relations with the followers of other religions. "Interreligious dialogue is part of the Church's evangelizing mission.... Dialogue is not in opposition to mission *ad gentes*; indeed, it has special links with that mission and is one of its expressions" (RM 55). "Each member of the faithful and all Christian communities are called to practice dialogue" (RM 57). Pope John Paul II was an indefatigable apostle of dialogue in his writings and world-wide pastoral visits, always taking an opportunity to meet the followers of various religions. He summoned the leaders of the world religions to assemble in Assisi in 1986, 1999, and 2002; Benedict XVI invited a return to Assisi in 2011, the twenty-fifth anniversary of the first Assisi gathering. The mission encyclical of John Paul II has a lengthy section devoted to interfaith dialogue (RM 55-57). His conviction was clear: "Interreligious dialogue is a part of the Church's evangelizing mission" (RM 55).

In Asia, where less than three percent of the population is Christian, the Church actively promotes interfaith dialogue. "Since the Council the Church has consistently shown that she wants to pursue that relationship in a spirit of dialogue.... The dialogue which the Church proposes is grounded in the logic of the Incarnation" (EA 29). "It is therefore important for the Church in Asia to provide suitable models of interreligious dialogue—evangelization in dialogue and dialogue for evangelization—and suitable training for those involved" (EA 31).

Asia's bishops are also deeply committed to dialogical evangelization; they have stated: "Mission may find its greatest urgency in Asia; it also finds in our continent a distinctive mode ... dialogue" (FABC V: 4.1). Being a truly local Church in Asia "means concretely [being] a Church in continuous, humble and loving dialogue with the living traditions, the cultures, the religions [of Asia]" (FABC I: 12). The Church has made significant progress in this area since Vatican II; however, as the world witnesses—almost daily—the need for authentic, substantial interfaith dialogue remains an urgent imperative. Effective and successful dialogue efforts are graces to be sought in prayer.

VIII. Foundational Mission Theology. Essential to an adequate appreciation of the waves of renewal in mission in the Vatican II era is a deepened comprehension of missiological foundations. Underlying the renewed approaches and concrete initiatives of mission one finds profound theological reflection. Particularly significant areas have been: Christology, Kingdom Theology, Pneumatology (cf. RM 4-30) as well as catholicity, the paschal mystery, and the triunity of God. Although not always grasped or appreciated by most Catholics, mission theologians have made a significant contribution to Church renewal.

In reference to foundational mission theology, one could reflect on the centrality of Christ in theology and missiology. The Second Vatican Council sought to link its teachings into the tradition of the Church through *ressourcement* (a return to foundational sources). It employed biblical language and had a clear focus on Christ and the Church. The Council recognized a clear "hierarchy of truths" that placed Christ the Son of God at its highest level (UR 11).

Paul VI spoke clearly of the centrality of Christ: "There can be no true evangelization if the name, the teaching, the life, the promises, the Kingdom and the mystery of Jesus of Nazareth, the Son of God, are not proclaimed" (EN 22). For John Paul II, the proclamation of the mystery of Christ "lies at the heart of the Church's mission and life, as the hinge on which all evangelization turns" (RM 44).

The Church in Asia declares: "To bear witness to Jesus Christ is the supreme service which the Church can offer to the peoples of Asia, for it responds to their profound longing for the Absolute, and it unveils the truths and values which will ensure their integral human development" (*Ecclesia in Asia* 20). The Church in Asia seeks to give credible witness to Christ: "Her one ambition is to continue his mission of service and love, so that all Asians 'may have life and have it abundantly' (Jn 10:10)" (EA 50).

Another example may suffice to illustrate how a renewed missiology has fostered the missionary growth and dynamism of the entire Church. Pneumatology, the theology of the Holy Spirit, has prospered since the Council. In *Evangelii Nuntiandi*, Pope Paul VI emphasized that "the Holy Spirit is the principal agent of evangelization" and that "evangelization will never be possible without the action of the Holy Spirit" (EN 75). Pope John Paul II elaborated upon the vision of Paul VI; one entire chapter of *Redemptoris Missio* (21-30) is devoted to the Spirit's role in mission. As noted earlier, John Paul II's mission vision has been significantly influenced by Vatican II; Catholics "ought to believe that the Holy Spirit in a manner known to God offers everyone the possibility of being associated with this paschal mystery" (GS 22; cf. RM 6, 10, 28). The theological foundations of mission contain great potential for the transformation of all Christians and their local Churches.

A third example would be the reflection of Vatican II on religious freedom. The promotion of evangelization actually presupposes a full acceptance of the Council document on religious freedom, *Dignitatis Humanae*. The Church asserts that "free exercise of religion in society" is a value "proper to the human spirit" (DH 1). All persons are encouraged to follow their responsible judgment in conscience without external pressure.

Paul VI is eloquent on this topic in *Evangelii Nuntiandi*: "It would certainly be an error to impose something on the consciences of our brethren. But to propose to their consciences the truth of the Gospel and salvation in Jesus Christ, with complete clarity and with total respect for the free options which it presents—'without coercion, or dishonorable or unworthy pressure'—far from being an attack on religious liberty is fully to respect that liberty, which is offered the choice of a way that even non-believers consider noble and uplifting" (EN 80).

Similarly, John Paul II affirms a respectful proclamation of the Gospel. "On her part, the Church addresses people with full respect for their freedom. Her mission does not restrict freedom but rather promotes it. *The Church proposes; she imposes nothing.* She respects individuals and cultures, and she honors the sanctuary of conscience" (RM 39).

The Church in Asia calls upon governments "to recognize religious freedom as a fundamental human right ... [and she invokes the words of Vatican II, noting] the human person has a right to religious freedom. Such freedom consists in this, that all should have such immunity from coercion by individuals, or by social groups, or by any human power, so that no one should be forced to act against his conscience in religious matters, nor prevented from acting according to his conscience, whether in private or in public, whether alone or in association with others, within due limits" (EA 23).

IX. Vision of Vatican II: Paradigm of a Missionary Church. Pope Benedict XVI, on April 20, 2005, the day after his election as Supreme Pontiff of the Roman Catholic Church, recalled the Second Vatican Council and noted its importance for the renewal of the Church and her mission. He forcefully stated: "Pope John Paul II rightly pointed out the Council as a 'compass' by which to take our bearings in the vast ocean of the third millennium…. I also wish to confirm my determination to continue to put the Second Vatican Council into practice…. As the years have passed the Conciliar documents have lost none of their timeliness; indeed, their teachings are proving particularly relevant to the new situation of the Church and the current globalized society" (OR-EE, 27-04-05, p. 3).

Pope John XXIII (canonized on April 27, 2014) asked the Church to read "the signs of the times" to fulfill her mission of evangelization; the pope asked for a "new Pentecost" and a renewed missionary spirit. Pope Paul VI noted in 1966: "One may say that the Council leaves itself as a legacy to the Church that held it." Paul VI also expressed a continual missionary challenge to the Church arising from Vatican II: "The first need of the Church is to always live Pentecost."

In 1975 Paul VI issued two interrelated apostolic exhortations: *Evangelii Nuntiandi* (Evangelization in the Modern World) and *Gaudete in Domino* (On Christian Joy). The pope constantly asserted that if the Gospel is not heard from "joyful evangelizers," it will not be heard at all by contemporary humanity. The lack of joy and hope is an obstacle to effective evangelization. Paul VI believed that joy would enable the world of our time "to receive the Good News not from evangelizers who are dejected, discouraged, impatient or anxious, but from ministers of the Gospel whose lives glow with fervor, who have first received the joy of Christ, and who are willing to risk their lives so that the Kingdom may be proclaimed and the Church established in the midst of the world" (EN 80).

The success of evangelization requires "renewed evangelizers." Jesuit Pierre Teilhard de Chardin wrote: "Joy is the most infallible sign of the presence of God." Joy is convincing; joy evangelizes. All the complex dimensions of evangelization will not overwhelm those whose lives have been transformed by a joyful encounter with the Risen Lord. As individuals and as a Church community, we must listen frequently to the admonition of Saint Paul: "Rejoice in the Lord always. I shall say it again: rejoice! Your kindness should be known to all. The Lord is near" (Gal 4:4). Be transformed by Christian joy.

Conclusion. One must explicitly state that this presentation is merely an *extended outline* and *brief commentary* on the renewal in *missionary vision and praxis* in the era of the Second Vatican Council. This presentation of nine defining traits that characterize evangelization may appear to readers to be overwhelming. Yes, the task of evangelization in the contemporary world is genuinely complex and awesomely challenging. Indeed, no individual can hope to accomplish any more than a small fragment of the total task. Thus, it is imperative that all segments of the Church collaborate in this beautiful endeavor, believing that, as John Paul II affirmed, "God is preparing a great springtime for Christianity" (RM 86).

Further elaboration is both desirable and necessary to appreciate how the Spirit has renewed the Church in and through the Council. How are the local Churches in Asia receiving this gift and task from the Council? Has there been a "missionary Pentecost"—especially in the Church in your own country?

The nine waves of mission renewal outlined here were initiated by the Second Vatican Council and they continue to enrich God's holy people, the Church; *they set the mission agenda for Asia in the third millennium*! Again and again, missioners can profitably reflect on a startling statement by Emil Brunner (quoted earlier): "The Church exists by mission as fire exists by burning." Become a herald of evangelization, announcing truly good news!

APPENDIX A:

MISSION MOTIVATION

The vastness of the Asian continent and its billions of peoples, the number, complexity and tenacity of its problems, the minority status of the Church, the many challenges to mission and missionaries—all these realities could cause paralysis and discouragement in Christians. The local Churches of Asia (and the missionaries who serve them) constantly need grounding and renewal in their motivation for mission. A creative expression of a renewed sense of mission is found in the FABC documents; five core motives can respond to the question: "Why evangelize?"

1. "We evangelize, first of all from a deep sense of *gratitude to God*, the Father 'who has blessed us in Christ with every spiritual blessing' (Eph 1:3).... Mission is above all else an overflow of this life from grateful hearts transformed by the grace of God. That is why it is so important ... to have a deep faith-experience of the love of God in Christ Jesus (Rom 8:39).... Without a personal experience of this love received as gift and mercy, no sense of mission can flourish" (FABC V, 3.2.1).

2. "But mission is also a *mandate*. We evangelize because we are sent into the whole world to make disciples of all nations. The one who sends us is Jesus.... He sends us on a mission which is part of the epiphany of God's plan to bring all things together under Christ as head (Eph 1:9-10). We cannot fulfill this mission apart from him (Jn 15:4-5)" (FABC V, 3.2.2). Asian Christians strive to take Christ's mission commands to heart, to go to the ends of the earth.

3. "We evangelize also because we *believe* in the Lord Jesus. We have received the gift of faith. We have become Christians.... Unfortunately for many Catholics, faith is only something to be received and celebrated. They do not feel it is something to be shared. The missionary nature of the gift of faith must be inculcated in all Christians" (FABC V, 3.2.3).

4. "We evangelize also because we have been *incorporated by baptism into the Church*, which is missionary by its very nature.... The Church exists in order to evangelize.... Each member, by virtue of the sacraments of baptism and

confirmation has received the right and duty to the apostolate from the Lord himself" (FABC V, 3.2.4).

5. "And, finally, we evangelize because the Gospel is *leaven* for liberation and for the transformation of society. Our Asian world needs the values of the Kingdom and of Christ in order to bring about the human development, justice, peace and harmony with God..." (FABC V, 3.2.5).

In addition to the motives for mission expressed by the FABC for the Asian context, one finds helpful insights for engagement in mission in John Paul II's *Ecclesia in Asia*, where, in many places, an incipient "gift missiology" appears. This author believes that mission viewed and practiced as an "exchange of gifts" is most appropriate for Asian peoples, their sensibilities, and values.

"The Church's faith in Jesus is a gift received and a gift to be shared; it is the greatest gift which the Church can offer to Asia. Sharing the truth of Jesus Christ with others is the solemn duty of all who have received the gift of faith" (EA 10b). "Blessed with the gift of faith, the Church, after two thousand years, continues to go out to meet the peoples of the world in order to share with them the Good News of Jesus Christ.... The great question now facing the Church in Asia is *how* to share with our Asian brothers and sisters what we treasure as the gift containing all gifts, namely, the Good News of Jesus Christ" (EA 19a, 19c).

John Paul II continues: "... the effort to share the gift of faith in Jesus as the only Savior is fraught with philosophical, cultural and theological difficulties, especially in light of the beliefs of Asia's great religions, deeply intertwined with cultural values and specific world views" (EA 20c). "Only if the People of God recognize the gift that is theirs in Christ will they be able to communicate that gift to others through *proclamation* and *dialogue*" (EA 31f).

ABBREVIATIONS

AA   - *Apostolicam Actuositatem* (Laity: November 18, 1965)

ABM   - Asian Bishops' Meeting (Manila: November 29, 1970)

ACMC   - Asian Colloquium on Ministries in the Church (Hong Kong, 1977)

AG   - *Ad Gentes* (Missionary Activity of the Church: December 7, 1965)

CD   - *Christus Dominus* (Bishops: October 28, 1965)

DH   - *Dignitatis Humanae* (Religious Freedom: December 7, 1965)

DV   - *Dei Verbum* (Divine Revelation: November 18, 1965)

EA   - *Ecclesia in Asia* (The Church in Asia: November 6, 1999)

EN   - *Evangelii Nuntiandi* (Evangelization Today: December 8, 1975)

FABC   - Federation of Asian Bishops' Conferences

FABC I - Evangelization in Modern Day Asia (Taipei, 1974)

FABC V - Journeying Together Toward the Third Millennium (Bandung, 1990)

FAPA   - *For All the Peoples of Asia: I* [1970-1991]; *For All the Peoples of Asia: II* [1992-1996]; *For All the Peoples of Asia: III* [1997-2001]; *For All the Peoples of Asia: IV* [2002-2006]; *For All the Peoples of Asia: V* [2007-2012]; edited by: Rosales, Gaudencio; Arévalo, Catalino; Eilers, Franz-Josef; and Tirimanna, Vimal. Maryknoll, NY: Orbis Books and Quezon City, Philippines: Claretian Publications: 1992, 1997, 2002, 2007, and 2014.

GD   - *Gaudete in Domino* (Christian Joy by Paul VI: May 9, 1975)

GS   - *Gaudium et Spes* (The Church in the Modern World: December 7, 1965)

IM   - *Inter Mirifica* (Social Communications: December 4, 1963)

LG   - *Lumen Gentium* (The Church: November 21, 1964)

NA   - *Nostra Aetate* (Non-Christian Religions: October 28, 1965)

OR-EE - *L'Osservatore Romano* (English Edition)
PO - *Presbyterorum Ordinis* (Priests: December 7, 1965)
RM - *Redemptoris Missio* (Church's Missionary Mandate: December 7, 1990)
SC - *Sacrosanctum Concilium* (Sacred Liturgy: December 4, 1963)
UR - *Unitatis Redintegratio* (Ecumenism: November 21, 1964)
UUS - *Ut Unum Sint* (That All Be One by John Paul II: May 25, 1995)

ASIAN PERSPECTIVES ON CHURCH AND MISSION
A Selected Bibliography

Benedict XVI. "World Mission Sunday 2011 Message," *See*: www.vatican.va.

Bevans, S. "Inculturation of Theology in Asia: The FABC 1970-1995," *Studia Missionalia* (Rome) 45 (1996): 1-23.

Champagne, C. "New Evangelization: New Challenges for the Church's Mission," *Origins* 37:22 (November 8, 2007): 341-347.

Chia, E. "Thirty Years of FABC: History, Foundation, Context and Theology," *FABC Papers 106* (2003): 1-55.

Colombo, D. (Ed.) *Documenti della Chiesa in Asia: Federazione delle Conferenze Episcopali Asiatiche (1970-1995)*. Bologna: Editrice Missionaria Italiana, 1997.

Darmaatmadja, C. "A Church with a Truly Asian Face," *Origins* 28:1 (May 21, 1998): 24-28.

Dulles, A. **(A)** "John Paul II and the New Evangelization," *Studia Missionalia* 48 (1999): 165-180; **(B)** *Evangelization for the Third Millennium*. New York: Paulist Press, 2009.

Dupuis, J. "FABC Focus on the Church's Evangelizing Mission in Asia Today," *Vidyajyoti* 56 (1992): 449-468; similar presentation in: *FABC Papers 64* (1992): 1-19.

Eilers, F-J. [**Rosales, G., Arévalo, C.G.**, and **Tirimanna, V.**] (Eds.). *For All the Peoples of Asia I-II-III-IV-V* [five volumes of FABC Documents]. Maryknoll, NY: Orbis Books and Quezon City, Philippines: Claretian Publications, 1992, 1997, 2002, 2007, and 2014.

Evers, G. "Challenges to the Churches in Asia Today," *East Asian Pastoral Review* 43 (2006): 152-172.

FABC Secretariat. *FABC Papers 1-141*. Hong Kong: FABC Secretariat, 1976-2014.

Kroeger, J. (**A**) "Introducing Asia's Mission Societies," *SEDOS Bulletin* 30:5 (1998): 141-144; (**B**) *The Future of the Asian Churches: The Asian Synod and Ecclesia in Asia* (edited with P. Phan). Quezon City, Philippines: Claretian Publications, 2002; (**C**) "A Church Living to Evangelize: Recent Popes and Integral Evangelization," in: *Becoming Local Church: Historical, Theological and Missiological Essays*. Quezon City, Philippines: Claretian Publications, 2003: 55-86; (**D**) *The Challenge of Religious Diversity in Migration*. Quezon City, Philippines: Scalabrini Migration Center, 2005; (**E**) "Mary, Mother of the Missionary Church," *Landas* 19:1 (2005): 19-35; (**F**) "Asia's Dynamic, Missionary Local Churches: FABC Perspectives," *Landas* 19:2 (2005): 175-207; (**G**) "The Faith-Culture Dialogue in Asia: Ten FABC Insights on Inculturation," *Studia Missionalia* 57 (2008): 91-115; see also: *Boletin Eclesiastico de Filipinas* 85:870 (2009): 7-28; (**H**) *Theology from the Heart of Asia: FABC Doctoral Dissertations I-II*. Quezon City, Philippines: Claretian Publications, 2008; (**I**) "Walking the Path of Dialogue in Asia: Insights from the FABC," *Studia Missionalia* 58 (2009): 45-77; (**J**) *FABC Papers 61, 88, 92o, 100, 107, 115, 117, 125, 130*. Hong Kong: FABC Secretariat, 1991-2010.

Latoza, J. "A Renewed Church in Asia: A Mission of Love and Service to Migrant Workers and Refugees in the Third Millennium," *FABC Papers 92f*. Hong Kong: FABC Secretariat, 2000.

Machado, F. "Interreligious Dialogue: An Essential Part of the Evangelizing Mission of the Church," *Euntes Docete* 57:1 (2004): 109-123.

Painadath, S. "Theological Perspectives of FABC on Interreligious Dialogue," *Jeevadhara* 27 (1997): 272-288.

Phan, P. (A) "Doing Theology in the Context of Cultural and Religious Pluralism: An Asian Perspective," *Louvain Studies* 27 (2002): 39-68; **(B)** "Reception of Vatican II in Asia: Historical and Theological Analysis," *Gregorianum* 83:2 (2002): 269-285; **(C)** *The Asian Synod: Text and Commentaries*. Maryknoll, New York: Orbis Books, 2002; **(D)** *Christianities in Asia* (Ed.). Oxford: Wiley-Blackwell, 2011.

Pieris, A. "An Asian Paradigm: Interreligious Dialogue and Theology of Religions," *The Month* 26 (1993): 129-134.

Poulet-Mathis, A. "Ecumenical and Interreligious Dialogue in Asia: Concerns and Initiatives of the Federation of Asian Bishops' Conferences," *FABC Papers 49* (1987): 10-28.

Rogers, A. (Ed.). **(A)** *Migrations: A Sign of the Times*. Kuala Lumpur: Migrants Services Secretariat of the National Office of Human Development, 2006; **(B)** *Asian Consultation on Harmony through Reconciliation*. Manila: FABC Office of Human Development, 2007.

Synod of Bishops. "The New Evangelization for the Transmission of the Christian Faith" (*Lineamenta* for 2012 Synod of Bishops). *See*: www.vatican.va

Tan, J. (A) "Theologizing at the Service of Life: The Contextual Theological Methodology of the FABC," *Gregorianum* 81

(2000): 541-575; see also: *FABC Papers 108*. Hong Kong: FABC Secretariat, 2003; **(B)** *"Missio Inter Gentes*: Towards a New Paradigm in the Mission Theology of the FABC," *FABC Papers 109*. Hong Kong: FABC Secretariat, 2004.

Tirimanna, V. (Ed.). **(A)** *Sprouts of Theology from the Asian Soil: Collection of TAC and OTC Documents*. Bangalore: Claretian Publications, 2007; **(B)** *Harvesting from the Asian Soil: Towards an Asian Theology*. Bangalore: Asian Trading Corporation, 2011.

Wilfred, F. "What the Spirit Says to the Churches (Rev. 2:7)" [various editors], *Vidyajyoti* 62 (1998): 124-133.

ASIA'S CHURCHES, THEOLOGY AND MISSION
Four Decades of FABC Growth and Service

Celebrating its fortieth or ruby anniversary (1972-2012), the Federation of Asian Bishops' Conferences (FABC) gathered in Vietnam for its Tenth Plenary Assembly from December 10-16, 2012. The venue for the working sessions was the spacious compound of the Catholic Diocese of Xuan Loc, located about a three-hour drive east of Ho Chi Minh City. For the bishops, clergy, religious, and faithful of Xuan Loc Diocese hosting this event was a wish come true, almost a "miracle." The closing ceremonies on December 16 were hosted by the Ho Chi Minh Archdiocese.

The participants of FABC X numbered 111. Among them were seven Asian cardinals: Gaudencio Borbon Rosales of Manila who served as Papal Envoy; Oswald Gracias of Mumbai, FABC Secretary General, Jean-Baptiste Pham Minh Mân of Ho Chi Minh; Telesphore Toppo of Ranchi; John Tong Hon of Hong Kong; Malcolm Ranjith of Colombo; and, Luis Antonio Tagle of Manila. In addition, there were 69 bishops and 35 priests, religious and laity. The theme of the assembly was: "FABC at Forty Years—Responding to the Challenges of Asia: New Evangelization."

The FABC has been the most influential body in the Asian Church since the Second Vatican Council; it has validly been seen to be "Asia's Continuing Vatican II." This continental assembly of Asian Church leaders emerged from the gathering of 180 Asian Bishops with Pope Paul VI in Manila in 1970. After this Asian Bishops' Meeting, proposals for a permanent structure which would connect the Catholic Bishops of Asia with each other and foster pastoral-missionary exchanges and interaction were forwarded to Rome. Pope Paul VI agreed to the proposals and gave the body his initial approval in 1972. Currently, the FABC encompasses 19 bishops' conferences (originally there were only 11) and 9 associate members; East Timor is the most recently incorporated bishops' conference. In total, FABC includes 29 Asian countries in its jurisdiction.

Opening Activities. During the initial Eucharist, Cardinal Rosales, Papal Legate, conveyed the wish of Pope Benedict XVI that the bishops of Asia "manifest, by their renewed strength and zeal, the love of Christ, the Church and the Gospel ... [and] foster human culture and diligently pursue dialogue among the peoples." At the public opening ceremony, welcome remarks and greetings were offered by various Church officials as well as by Vietnamese Government Representatives.

The first major agenda item focused on a panoramic *historical review* of the FABC journey over the past four decades (since many younger bishops have limited knowledge of FABC origins). The content of the 1970 bishops' meeting with Paul VI in Manila was reviewed. The series of early follow-up meetings was recounted. The roles of various pivotal figures were mentioned, particularly Bishop Francis Hsu of Hong Kong and Korean Cardinal Stephen Kim, who is often called the "Father of FABC." It was Cardinal Kim along with two other FABC pioneers who took the initial proposals to Rome and personally asked Paul VI for his blessing and approval, provisionally granted in 1972.

Father Raymond Ambroise, executive secretary of the FABC Office of Social Communication, briefly shared the highlights of his lengthy paper on the history, vision, membership, structure, function, and activities of the FABC and each of its nine offices (Human Development; Social Communication; Laity and Family; Theological Concerns; Education and Faith Formation; Ecumenical and Interreligious Affairs; Evangelization; Clergy; and, Consecrated Life). A helpful synopsis of the previous nine plenary assemblies was also presented. The FABC website is home to a plethora of information about these matters.

Maryknoll Father James Kroeger highlighted the past four decades of "FABC theologizing" by providing a brief review of ten pivotal themes that are woven into FABC literature and documents. The theological underpinnings of the FABC vision of the local Church and its evangelizing mission are pivotal for an in-depth appreciation of the unique role FABC plays in Asia. Kroeger highlighted such themes as the "pastoral spiral methodology," laity and innovative pastoral ministries, as well as the famed FABC "triple dialogue" with Asia's people (especially the poor), cultures, and religions. NOTE: Please consult the helpful synopsis version of this presentation which is included here as *Appendix A*: "Four Decades of FABC Theology."

Major Document. The Presider at the Eucharist on the second working day of the assembly was Vietnam's Cardinal Jean-Baptiste Pham Minh Mân. He noted the many losses of the Vietnamese people after 1975 as well as the many new freedoms they experience today. He mentioned three anchors that guide his pastoral ministry. "I keep firm faith in Jesus, listening and keeping His Word in my heart." He continues to cooperate with the Holy Spirit, who "is working to renew our mind and open our heart to respond to the challenges of social life." The cardinal always looks to "the example of our Blessed Mother and our martyrs." In this way he hopes to respond to "so many people in need of the living water of Christ."

The major task of the day was to review, critique, and augment the assembly working paper written by Archbishop Orlando Quevedo of Cotabato, Philippines; the process unfolded in plenary as well as in regional sub-group sessions. The 30-page text is based on the theme of FABC X: "FABC at Forty Years—Responding to the Challenges of Asia: New Evangelization." The document has four sections. Section One outlines FABC history and highlights the theme of every previous plenary assembly. Section Two examines 15 "megatrends" that "shape the evangelizing mission of the Church in Asia": globalization, culture, poverty, migrants and refugees, indigenous peoples, population, religious freedom, threats to life, social communication, ecology, laity, women, youth, Pentecostalism, and vocations. The next section of the text offers a theological basis for the Church's proclamation and evangelizing mission. Lastly, the document briefly outlines the prophetic role of the Church dedicated to a "new evangelization" based upon the FABC's understanding of "a new way of being Church in Asia."

Special Interventions. Throughout the assembly time was made available for a variety of interventions coming from individuals within the member Episcopal conferences. Archbishop Leo Jun Ikenaga of Osaka, Japan highlighted the natural and human-made threats to life, citing in particular the destruction wrought by the 2011 earthquake and tsunami as well as the compounded problems that the crippled Fukushima nuclear plant inflicted on the Japanese people. In a moving testimony, Korean Bishop Peter Kang U-il of Cheju apologized to the Vietnamese people for the 5,000 civilians whom Korean troops summarily executed between 1968 and 1974. The bishop also recalled that, based on various sources, the South Korean forces also killed more than 40,000 Vietnamese in military actions.

Archbishop Savio Hon Tai-Fai, the Secretary of the Congregation for the Evangelization of Peoples in Rome, addressed the assembly concerning the current situation of the Church in China. Father Roberto M. Ebisa, SVD, General Manager of Radio Veritas Asia, made a comprehensive report on the status, progress, and changes of this FABC "voice of evangelization." Fraternal delegates from three Episcopal conferences (Europe, Latin America, and Oceania) expressed their appreciation for collaboration with the FABC. Delegates from mission partners and funding agencies (*Missio* and *Miserior*) described current realities affecting their relationship with FABC. The delegate from Timor Leste noted how their episcopal conference has been assisted by the vision of FABC. The assembly was enriched by the voices of the bishops from the Central Asian Republics and those of brother-bishops of the Syro-Malabar and Syro-Malankara Bishops' Conferences from India. Present also was Archbishop Leopoldo Girelli who is the Holy See's non-residential pontifical representative for Vietnam.

The assembly gave special recognition to Sister Mary Walter Santer, OSU, current executive secretary of the Office of Consecrated Life, for her more than three decades of dedicated service to FABC; as she approaches retirement, the plenary assembly body affectionate noted her generosity of spirit and her close collaboration with Father Edward Malone, MM, who served as the first FABC assistant secretary general for over thirty years.

Reports and Business Matters. The celebrant of the Eucharist on the third working-day of the conference was Cardinal John Tong Hon of Hong Kong, who said: "May I ask your prayers to bring us help to resolve the difficulties encountered in China-Vatican relations?" The cardinal noted that it is "a blessing for the FABC and for the universal Church" to hold an "important" gathering of the Asian Church in Vietnam. He continued: "This is a breakthrough in relations, and the result of much promising dialogue between the Church in Vietnam and the Vatican, and between the Vietnamese government and the Holy See.... I hope one day that the FABC assembly can take place in mainland China. [But] before reaching this goal, the issue of the appointment of bishops in China must first be resolved because some bishops in China are still illegitimate. Thus a dialogue between China and the Holy See is urgently needed."

The morning of the third day of the assembly was given to discussions by the nine regional groupings with the task of studying the megatrends affecting the Church's mission of evangelization in Asia; the trends were evaluated and additional ideas surfaced. These discussion groups were also to focus on concrete pastoral imperatives needed in the local Churches and across Asia. It was foreseen that the collated results of these discussions would be added as pastoral recommendations to the main text, as it went through refinement during the week-long assembly.

The afternoon of this third day was given to reports by the nine FABC Offices. Each Office prepared a written report of its activities since the 2009 IX Plenary Assembly held in Manila; the verbal report sought only to highlight the most significant activities of the offices in the years 2009-2012 [FABC plenary assemblies are normally held every four years]. As was practiced on the previous two evenings, the day concluded with the solemn and reverent Taizé Night Prayer in the presence of the Blessed Sacrament.

Recommendations. Cardinal Malcolm Ranjith presided at a simple Eucharist on the fourth working day of the assembly. The bulk of the day's sessions was spent on discussing, augmenting, and refining the two assembly documents: the Message and the Final Document. Of special interest are the ten recommendations added to the Final Document; they were selected from a variety of material emerging from the regional discussion groups. One recommendation was forthcoming on the topics of faith formation, poverty, threats to life, dialogue and peace, indigenous peoples, and the availability of the FABC documents; two recommendations were made on the topics of ecology and migrants and itinerant peoples.

Two examples will suffice to portray the nature of the pastoral recommendations. On the topic of poverty, the FABC noted: "That local churches promoting a culture of evangelical poverty, foster among all pastoral agents a deep concern for the poor so as to credibly witness to the Lord Jesus who had a preferential love for the poor." Another recommendation asserts: "That Episcopal conferences, particular and local churches make available the FABC Plenary Assembly documents in local languages so the thinking of Asian Bishops regarding the renewal of the Church may be accessible to our people."

A heartfelt commitment concludes the Final Document; it reads: "In this Year of Faith and on the fortieth anniversary of the FABC we firmly commit ourselves and our resources to the Church's mission of New Evangelization—to proclaim Jesus as the Lord and tell his story to the peoples of Asia with new ardor, new methods and new expressions." An impressive and thoroughly enjoyable cultural evening concluded the day.

Final Message. As the assembly drew to its conclusion, the bishops approved the Message to the People of God; the well-framed document was the result of the dedication of Father Jacob Theckanath, principal drafter. The beautiful title superbly captures the spirit of the week-long prayerful reflections: "Renewed Evangelizers for New Evangelization in Asia." One finds much inspiration in the document: "This has truly been a Week of Faith." "At the core of the New Evangelization … is the clarion call to be authentic and credible witnesses of Jesus the Lord and Savior." "We need to live a spirituality of New Evangelization." "If we exist for mission, we need to have a passion for mission." "May Mary, the Mother of Jesus and our Mother, accompany us as we walk the roads of Asia, to 'tell the story of Jesus'." NOTE: Due to the importance of the "Message of Tenth FABC Plenary Assembly" and its modest size, the full text is included here as *Appendix B*.

Conclusion and Gratitude. Having completed the working sessions on the fifth day of the assembly, the participants traveled back to Ho Chi Minh City, where everyone was hosted for a Saturday-evening Eucharist by fourteen different city parishes. The closing Eucharist, presided by Cardinal Oswald Gracias, was held in the majestic Ho Chi Minh City Cathedral on December 16, Third Sunday of Advent. Selections of the Final Message were read at the conclusion of the Eucharist; several messages of gratitude were also delivered. With particular affection Cardinal Gracias thanked Cardinal Pham Minh Mân, whom he called the "Patriarch of the Church in Vietnam." Cardinal Mân hosted a closing lunch at his residence.

Participants of Tenth FABC Plenary Assembly were at a loss for words to adequately express their gratitude for the exquisite hospitality and preparations made to assure the success of this first major international gathering of the Catholic Church in Vietnam in several decades. Delegates lauded the efficiency and generosity of the local Church, its leaders and the many fervent laity. The friendship and openness of the Vietnamese people were warmly received and then reciprocated. Everyone witnessed and praised the vibrant spiritual life of the Church in Vietnam. The entire Church in Asia—in fact, the Universal Church—stands to be greatly enriched and blessed by the many gifts the Local Church in Vietnam has to give and share.

APPENDIX A:

FOUR DECADES OF FABC THEOLOGY
Pivotal Characteristics and Emphases

James H. Kroeger, MM

Many approaches are possible when one attempts to capture the growth and evolution of "FABC theologizing" since the historic meeting of Pope Paul VI with 180 Asian bishops in Manila in November 1970. One helpful attempt to present this corpus of material would be to chronicle the "ten FABC plenary assemblies" with their profound insights. A second approach would be to trace the "movements toward a renewed Church in Asia" as was done in the FABC VII final document [*For All the Peoples of Asia (FAPA) III*: 3-4]. Thirdly, various theologians have identified "pivotal themes"; see C. Arévalo and F. Wilfred [*FAPA I*: xv-xxii], S. Bevans [*FABC Papers 78*] and E. Chia [*FABC Papers 106*]. Fourthly, one could explore the numerous "doctoral dissertations" written on various FABC key themes in the 40-year "historical-theological-pastoral-missionary" FABC journey [*Theology from the Heart of Asia: I-II; FABC Papers 125*: 45-48]. Based on consultation with some "FABC Fathers," this brief presentation highlights ten focuses that lie at the heart of FABC Theology. In a word, this paper employs "pivotal theological currents" to capture the forty-year FABC historical evolution.

I. Inductive Approach and Pastoral Spiral Methodology. Generally, FABC theologizing begins in the concrete context, endeavoring to explore life's realities as the locus of doing theology. In their 1970 meeting the Asian bishops noted their sincere efforts "to open our minds and hearts to the needs and aspirations of our peoples ... [and] to look upon the face of Asia" [*FAPA I*: 3]. The FABC Office of Theological Concerns issued its lengthy "Methodology: Asian Christian Theology (Doing Theology in Asia Today)" in 2000 [*FAPA III*: 329-419; *FABC Papers 96*]. BISA VII (1986) enunciated the "Pastoral Cycle," (later renamed the "Pastoral Spiral") which is comprised of four stages: *first*: exposure and immersion; *second*: social analysis and an examination of the "human impact" of life's realities upon people; *third*: the contemplative dimension which seeks to "discover God's presence and activity within social reality"; and, *fourth*: pastoral planning which "seeks to translate the previous three stages into actual, realizable plans" [*FAPA I*: 229-233]. The FABC has widely promoted the AsIPA method (Asian Integral Pastoral Approach) as one way to foster the growth of a participatory and co-responsible Church through the development of basic ecclesial communities; an AsIPA Desk within the Office of Laity and Family was established in late 1993. The inductive theological approach was once again employed in the Tenth Plenary Assembly (2012) as it explored "mega-trends in Asia" as the best way of "responding to the challenges of Asia" and fostering a "new evangelization."

II. Jesus' Vision of the Reign of God within an Asian Context. For the Asian bishops, "seeking the Kingdom of God that Jesus proclaimed is really to build it in the concrete experiences of the social, political, economic, religious and cultural world of Asia.... The struggle for fullness of life in Asia is a seeking of the Kingdom" [*FAPA I*: 196]. In a 1991 theological consultation sponsored by the FABC Office of Evangelization, it was noted: "The Kingdom of God is ... universally present and at work. Wherever men and women open themselves to the transcendent divine mystery which impinges upon them and go out of themselves in love and service to fellow humans, there the Reign of God is a universal reality, extending far beyond the boundaries of the Church" [*FAPA I*: 341]. Again, it is asserted: "Therefore, we commit ourselves: ... To take every opportunity to make Jesus Christ and his message known in a way that is acceptable to Asians, presenting him to them with an 'Asian face,' using Asian cultural concepts, terms, and symbols; ... To present the Gospel message as humble servants of the Kingdom of God, always sensitive to the religious and cultural traditions of the people where the Spirit leads us to make Jesus known" [*FAPA III*: 206].

III.   Local Church as Primary Actor. The First FABC Plenary Assembly (1974) stated: "The primary focus of our task of evangelization then, at this time in our history, is the building up of a truly local church. For the local church is the realization and the enfleshment of the Body of Christ in a given people, a given place and time.... The local church is a church incarnate in a people, a church indigenous and inculturated. And this means concretely a church in continuous, humble and loving dialogue with the living traditions, the cultures, the religions...." [FABC I: 9-12; *FAPA I*: 14]. FABC V (1990) asserted that "the acting subject of mission is the *local church* living and acting in communion with the universal Church. It is the local churches and communities which can discern and work out (in dialogue with each other and with other persons of goodwill) the way the Gospel is best proclaimed, the Church set up, the values of God's Kingdom realized in their own place and time. In fact, it is by responding to and serving the needs of the people of Asia that the different Christian communities become truly local churches. This local church, which is the acting subject of mission, is the people of God in a given milieu, the whole Christian community—laity, Religious and clergy. It is the whole diocese, the parish, the Basic Ecclesial Community and other groups. Their time has come for Asia" [FABC V: 3.3.1-2; *FAPA I*: 281].

IV. Dialogue as the Mode of Presence in Asian Contexts. Asia is a continent rich in diverse faith traditions; 85% of all the world's non-Christians live in Asia. Asia's bishops have a deep appreciation of the role of dialogue in the evangelization process; they hold: "Interreligious dialogue is another integral part of evangelization which in the situation of our Churches needs to become a primary concern. We live in the midst of

millions of people belonging to the great religious traditions.…
In this context we believe that interreligious dialogue is a true
expression of the Church's evangelizing action in which the
mystery of Jesus Christ is operative, calling us all to conversion"
[*FAPA I*: 100-101]. "The Church, the sacrament of God's
message in the world, continues Christ's work of dialogue.…
The Christian finds himself continually evangelizing and
being evangelized by his partners in dialogue" [*FAPA I*: 115].
"Mission may find its greatest urgency in Asia: it also finds in our
continent a distinctive mode [dialogue]" [*FAPA I*: 281]. FABC
III (1982) sought to promote "a true and real 'dialogue of life'
with one another" in the Asian context [*FAPA I*: 64]. "Dialogue
does not call for giving up one's commitment, bracketing it or
entering into easy compromise. On the contrary, for a deeper
and fruitful dialogue, it is even necessary that each partner be
firmly committed to his or her faith" [*FAPA I*: 309-310]. See
also: "Dialogue: Interpretive Key for the Life of the Church in
Asia," [*FABC Papers 130*].

V. Interiority and Motivation for Mission. FABC II (1978),
with its theme "Prayer—The Life of the Church in Asia," [*FAPA
I*: 27-48], focused on the need for deep spirituality in the Asian
Church. There must be "contact with the living God"; "prayer
commits us to the true liberation of persons. It binds us to
solidarity with the poor and the powerless" [*FAPA I*: 31, 33].
FABC V (1990) enunciated an Asian perspective on "motivation
for mission," seeking to answer the perennial question: Why
should we evangelize? Five motives are noted: "We evangelize,
first of all, from a deep sense of *gratitude to God*.… Mission
is above all else an overflow of this life from grateful hearts
transformed by the grace of God.… Without a personal
experience of this love received as gift and mercy, no sense
of mission can flourish. But mission is also a *mandate*. We
evangelize because we are sent into the whole world to make
disciples of all nations.… We evangelize also because we *believe*
in the Lord Jesus. We have received the gift of faith.… We
evangelize also because we have been *incorporated by baptism
into the Church*, which is missionary by its very nature.… And
finally, we evangelize because the Gospel is *leaven* for liberation

and for the transformation of society [FABC V: 3:2; *FAPA I*: 280-281]. FABC IX in Manila (2009) focused its entire attention on the Eucharist and its pivotal role in Christian life; see *Living the Eucharist in Asia [FABC Papers 129]*.

VI. Mission: Announcing the Person and Promises of Christ. The Churches of Asia see a clear Christological component to evangelization; they assert: "While we are aware and sensitive to the fact that evangelization is a complex realty and has many essential aspects ... we affirm that there can never be true evangelization without the proclamation of Jesus Christ. The proclamation of Jesus Christ is the center and the primary element of evangelization without which all other elements will lose their cohesion and validity" [*FAPA I*: 292]. During FABC V (Bandung, 1990), Asia's bishops stated: "We affirm ... that 'the proclamation of Jesus Christ is the center and primary element of evangelization.' ... But the proclamation of Jesus Christ in Asia means, first of all, the witness of Christians and Christian communities to the values of the Kingdom of God, *a proclamation through Christ-like deeds.* For Christians in Asia, to proclaim Christ means above all to live like him, in the midst of our neighbors of other faiths and persuasions, and to do this by the power of his grace. Proclamation through dialogue and deeds—this is the first call to the Churches in Asia" [*FAPA I*: 281-282]. Thus, "the local Churches of Asia will proclaim Jesus Christ to their fellow humans in a dialogical manner" [*FAPA I*: 346].

VII. Role of Laity in a "New Way of Being Church." FABC IV (Tokyo, 1986) focused on "The Vocation and Mission of the Laity in the Church and in the World of Asia" [*FAPA I*: 177-198]. This FABC assembly explored the role of laity in such areas as politics, youth, women, family, education, mass media, health services, work and business, identifying these areas as "the signs of the times" which are to "be discerned by Christians and the Church of Asia." FABC VI asserted: "It is in the faith response we give these challenges that we will discern and discover the vocation and mission of the laity for the salvation of Asia.... Such a commitment by all Christians will make the Church a communion of committed disciples—be they clergy or laity—working for the liberation of Asia" [*FAPA I*: 191]. FABC VIII (Daejeon, Korea, 2004) reflected deeply on the Asian Family [*FAPA IV*: 1-61]. One may note that the FABC Office of Laity and Family has three specialized desks (women, AsIPA, and youth) linked into its wide areas of concern.

VIII. Engagement with and the Evangelization of Cultures. FABC I (Taipei, 1974) asserted that the Church in Asia must become "a Church incarnate in a people, a Church indigenous and inculturated. And this means concretely a church in continuous, humble and loving dialogue with the living traditions, the cultures, the religions—in brief, with all the life-realities of the people in whose midst it has sunk its roots deeply and whose history and life it gladly makes its own. It seeks to share in whatever truly belongs to that people: its meanings and its values, its aspirations, its thoughts and its language, its songs and its artistry—even its frailties it assumes, so that they too may be healed. For so did God's Son assume the totality of our fallen human condition (save only for sin) so that He might make it truly His own, and redeem it in His paschal mystery" [*FAPA I*: 14]. In fact, the Asian Bishops' Meeting in 1970 had already spoken of "the inculturation of the life and message of the Gospel in Asia" which will flow from "a deep respect for the culture and traditions of our peoples" [*FAPA I*: 6]. This dialogue with cultures forms one dimension of the famed FABC "triple dialogue." An in-depth "faith-culture" dialogue is pivotal for understanding the challenges of the new evangelization!

IX. Faith-motivated Liberating Engagement in Society. The Office of Human Development, considered to be the first FABC Office (1971), helped focus attention on the social needs of the majority of Asian people who are poor; its emphasis was heavily influenced by the 1970 visit of Paul VI to Asia and his *Populorum Progressio* (1967). The Asian Bishops (1970) noted: "It is our resolve, first of all, to be more truly 'the Church of the poor' [and to] place ourselves at the side of the multitudes in our continent" [*FAPA I*: 5]. The Sixth FABC Plenary Assembly in Manila (1995—25 years after the 1970 gathering of the Asian Bishops with Pope Paul in Manila) explored the meaning of Christian discipleship in Asia. The assembly identified "five concerns that require pastoral focus": the Asian family, women and the girl-child, the youth, ecology, and the displaced (refugees and migrants) [*FAPA II*: 10-12].

X. Promotion of Innovative Pastoral Ministries. The FABC-sponsored "Asian Colloquium on Ministries in the Church" (1977) saw the need to create "new forms of ministries, alongside the existing ones ... [because] the servant Church can never adequately exercise her ministeriality through one uniform type of ministry" [*FAPA I*: 78]. The colloquium deepened the Church's awareness that as she is lead by her servant Lord, she "has to discover time and again what ministries and ministerial structures she requires in order to fulfill her mission to offer to a human society the salvation brought about by Jesus Christ and to enable the members of that society to become what God intends them to be" [*FAPA I*: 72]. The assembly proceeded to identify over a dozen possible specialized ministries [*FAPA I*: 78-81]. These innovations will enable Asian Churches to "become truly Asian in all things" [*FAPA I*: 72].

Synthesis: Diagram of the FABC Paradigm of Evangelization. For four decades (1972-2012) Asia's Christian communities have been striving to build an "evangelizing Church" in Asia (expressed in the following "triple dialogue" diagram):

		ASIA'S PEOPLE (POOR)
LOCAL CHURCH	<< DIALOGUE >>	ASIA'S CULTURES
(subject)	(mode)	ASIA'S RELIGIONS

This paradigm of missionary evangelization in Asia was initially enunciated in the First FABC Plenary Assembly in 1974. It struck a deep chord with Asia's bishops and Christian communities, precisely because it captures the mind and mission of the local Churches, who struggle to be "in continuous, humble and loving dialogue with the living traditions, the cultures, the religions—in brief, with all the life-realities of the people" [*FAPA I*: 14]. In FABC V (1990) the vision was reaffirmed: "Mission will mean a dialogue with Asia's poor, with its local cultures, and with other religious traditions" [*FAPA I*: 280]. FABC VII (2000) again reaffirmed the "triple dialogue," noting that "this is the vision of a renewed Church that the FABC has developed over the past thirty years. It is still valid today" [*FAPA III*: 4]. The Tenth FABC Plenary Assembly (2012) once again in its final document (No. 11) noted the local Church must be "truly Asian, in triple dialogue with the religions, cultures and peoples of Asia, especially the poor." FABC X also noted: "We thank the Lord for a challenging vision of Church in Asia."

APPENDIX B:

RENEWED EVANGELIZERS FOR NEW EVANGELIZATION IN ASIA
Message of Tenth FABC Plenary Assembly

"We declare to you what we have seen and heard" (I John 1:3)

We, the Bishops representing member-Episcopal Conferences and Associate Members of the Federation of Asian Bishops' Conferences gathered in Xuan Loc and Ho Chi Minh City, Vietnam, from 10 to 16 December 2012, for the Tenth Plenary Assembly of the Federation of the Asian Bishops' Conferences. With us were: the Holy Father's Special Envoy, Gaudencio Cardinal Rosales; the Secretary of the Congregation for the Evangelization of Peoples, Archbishop Savio Hon Tai-Fai SDB; the non-resident Pontifical representative to Vietnam, Archbishop Leopoldo Girelli; fraternal delegates of the continental Federations of Episcopal Conferences of Oceania, Latin America and Europe; representatives of a few funding and donor partners; the Bishops and Secretaries of the FABC Offices; and invited guests. There were a total of 111 participants (7 Cardinals, 69 Bishops, 35 priests, religious and laity).

We thank the Lord for the historic approval of the *Statutes* of the FABC 40 years ago. What extraordinary blessing it is for us that four important events converge with the FABC ruby anniversary: the Year of Faith, the 50th anniversary of the opening of the Second Vatican Council, the 20th anniversary of the publication of the *Catechism of the Catholic Church*, and the just concluded XIII Ordinary General Assembly of the Synod of Bishops on the New Evangelization for the Transmission of the Christian Faith.

All these events awaken us to our deepest identity—we are a community of faith called by the Lord to a mission of evangelization in the world. We thank the Lord for blessing the FABC in its ongoing work of renewing the mission of love and service in Asia.

We are deeply grateful for the exceedingly warm welcome and hospitality extended to us by the Church in Vietnam, particularly in Xuan Loc and Ho Chi Minh City. We thank the Government of Vietnam for its openness to, and support for, our gathering in this country blessed with rich cultures and traditions. We wish God's special blessings upon the Church in Vietnam and all the people of Vietnam.

We also express our communion and solidarity with, and encouragement for, the Catholic Church in China. We missed the presence of its representatives in our Assembly and we dearly hope that one day we would have a wider fellowship with their active participation in the FABC. We are united with them in prayer that the peace, joy and hope that Christ came to bring may reach all in that great country.

We convey our deep gratitude to all the Laity, men and women in Consecrated Life, Priests and Bishops who carry out the mission of evangelization in the most difficult situations even at the risk of their lives. Their courage for the Lord's Gospel and their dedication greatly edify and inspire us.

This has been truly a Week of Faith. Our faith in the Lord has been stirred into flame by the deep and lively faith of the people in the Church in Vietnam and by the story of their martyrs. Through the supreme witnessing of martyrs, the power of faith and hope shines forth.

In the light of the Word, our Plenary Assembly discerned the paths of mission to which the Spirit of God is beckoning us. Guided by the Spirit we read the signs of the times, the social mega-trends in Asia and our own ecclesial realities, and analyzed the unfolding challenges and opportunities so that we might respond to them from the depths of our faith. We have the daunting mission of proclaiming Jesus as the Lord and Savior amid rapid changes in Asia. For this reason we are ever more aware that we need to be a more Christ-experiencing and Christ-witnessing community. At the core of the New Evangelization initiated by Blessed Pope John Paul II and reiterated by Pope Benedict XVI is the clarion call to be authentic and credible witnesses of Jesus the Lord and Savior.

The same Spirit who animated Vatican II now summons us to become **renewed evangelizers for a New Evangelization**. It is the Spirit who can fashion this newness in our Church and in each one of us. It is the Spirit who enables us to respond credibly and effectively to the social mega-trends and ecclesial realities that our Assembly has discerned.

To be renewed as evangelizers we have to respond to the Spirit active in the world, in the depths of our being, in the signs of the times and in all that is authentically human. *We need to live a spirituality of New Evangelization*.

For such spirituality, we offer you some fundamental dimensions:

1. Personal Encounter with Jesus Christ. New

evangelizers need first and foremost a living faith that is grounded in a deep, personal, and transforming encounter with the living person of Jesus Christ, an encounter resulting in personal conversion and discipleship of Jesus in word and deed. In the final analysis, we proclaim the one whom we have seen, whom we have heard and touched (see *1 John* 1:1-3). This personal encounter and discipleship is indispensable. Without it none will be able to touch the soul of Asia.

2. Passion for Mission. If we exist for mission, we need to have a passion for mission. The story of the Church in Asia is intertwined with the story of missionaries and martyrs—laymen and women, consecrated persons and clergy—who dared to risk their lives for the sake of Christ. Their story inspires and emboldens us. They epitomize the passion for mission in a manner that is impossible for human beings, but possible for God (cf. *Luke* 18:27). Blessed Pope John Paul II affirmed, "A fire can only be lit by something that is itself on fire… (we) have to be on fire with the love of Christ and burning with zeal to make him known more widely, loved more deeply, and followed more closely" (*Ecclesia in Asia*, 23). The words of St. Paul move our hearts: "the charity of Christ urges us" (*2 Corinthians* 5:14) to share the unique love of Jesus with the whole world. For we firmly believe that the aspirations of Asian peoples find their ultimate fulfillment in Jesus, who is Life.

3. Focus on the Kingdom of God. The proclamation of Jesus affects every aspect of life and stratum of society— the whole of human life. Hence the spirituality of the new evangelizer does not separate our world from God's Reign. It does not separate the material from the religious, nor does it divorce faith-life from the task of transforming the socioeconomic and political life. Above all, the spirituality of the new evangelizer does not separate Jesus Christ from the Kingdom, nor detach the values of the Kingdom from the Person of Jesus. To focus on the Kingdom of God is to commit oneself to Jesus and His vision of a new humanity patterned after Him.

4. Commitment to Communion. Jesus prayed for us that we might be in communion with the Father, with him and with one another (cf. *John* 17:20-22). Through his Passion, Death, and Resurrection, he restored all things to himself and brought humanity and all creation to communion with the Father and the Spirit. Like Jesus, new evangelizers should be men and women who live and promote communion. ***The spirituality of communion is, in truth, the spirituality of the New Evangelization***. Blessed Pope John Paul II reminds us that "communion and mission are inseparably connected." Communion with the Triune God is "both the source and fruit of mission: communion gives rise to mission and mission is accomplished in communion" (*Ecclesia in Asia*, 24, citing *Christifideles Laici*, 32). This then should be our motto: "communion for mission" and the "mission of communion" (*Ecclesia in Asia*, 25). Evangelizers will be effective to the extent that they live a deep contemplative communion with Jesus and commit themselves generously to being witnesses and promoters of communion with God, with one another, and with creation.

In the Asian quest for harmony amid increasing tensions and conflicts, all members of the Church—clergy and laity, men and women, youth and children—are called to be evangelizers, heralds of the Word, peacemakers, and builders of communion. Such a communion expresses itself in a vibrant communion of communities in our parishes and dioceses.

5. Dialogue, a Mode of Life and Mission. The New Evangelization calls for a spirit of dialogue that animates daily living and opts for a unifying, rather than adversarial, relationship. Dialogue has to be a hallmark of all forms of ministry and service in Asia. It is characterized by humble sensitivity to the hidden presence of God in the struggles of the poor, in the riches of people's cultures, in the varieties of religious traditions, and in the depths of every human heart. Such dialogue is our mode of life and our mode of mission. It is fundamental to a spirituality of communion for the renewed evangelizer.

6. Humble Presence. We believe that everyone in Asia is a partner and co-pilgrim in the journey to God's Reign, that the fields of mission are grounds of the mysterious presence and action of God's Spirit. In the vast mission in Asia the silent but eloquent witness of an authentic Christian life requires a humble presence, a mode of dialogical living that includes a prayerful and "contemplative" way of life. This is imperative for renewed evangelizers amid cultures that value self-effacement and prayer. Humble presence must be matched by simplicity of life and communion with the poor.

7. Prophetic Evangelizer. To be prophetic is to be aware in the light of the Holy Spirit of the contradictions of our Asian world and to denounce whatever diminishes, degrades and divests God's children of their dignity. The renewed evangelizer has to protect the human dignity of all, especially of women and children and of those reduced to the condition of living almost as non-persons in our Asian society. By so denouncing injustice, the renewed evangelizer announces the love of God, "the weightier matters of the law" which are justice, mercy and faith (*Matthew* 23:23), and Jesus' preferential love of the poor.

8. Solidarity with Victims. We have noted in our Assembly that the number of victims of globalization, injustice, natural and nuclear disasters, and of attacks by fundamentalists and terrorists, is growing by the day. Jesus took the side of victims of disasters and injustices. He was in solidarity with those cast out of the social mainstream. Solidarity with and compassion for victims and the marginalized has to be an essential dimension of the spirituality for renewed evangelizers.

9. Care of Creation. Our Assembly has likewise noted the unabated abuse of creation due to selfish and shortsighted economic gains. Human causes contribute significantly to global warming and climate change, the impact of which affects the poor and the deprived more disastrously. The ecological concern, the care for the integrity of creation, including inter-generational justice and compassion, is fundamental to a spirituality of communion.

10. Boldness of Faith and Martyrdom. From the beginning of Christianity until now Asia's soil is marked by the blood of martyrs. If today we are called to give witness to our faith by supreme sacrifice, we are not to recoil. Jesus has forewarned us that such a sacrifice is the ultimate sign of total fidelity to him and his mission. Let the martyrs of our lands, many of whom are celebrated at our altars, inspire us by their example and empower us with their intercession. We are grateful to Blessed Pope John Paul II and Pope Benedict XVI for proclaiming many Asian witnesses to Christ as martyrs of the Church. Indeed, *"the blood of martyrs is the seed of Christianity."*

Conclusion. In this Year of Faith, in the second decade of the new millennium, and on the occasion of the 40th anniversary of the FABC, we appeal to all in the Church in Asia to nurture a special passion for New Evangelization.

We should not be led into lethargy or pessimism by Asian social mega-trends which threaten the fabric of our society, the stability of the family and the faith-vision of the Christian community itself. Hidden in them might be the inner resources of the Spirit veiled within Asian values, the seeds of a new humanity hungering for fullness of life in Jesus.

The mission of new evangelization, new in its ardor, its methods and its expressions, is urgent. It calls for renewed evangelizers with a renewed spirituality, the spirituality of communion, of mission, of new evangelization. Every parish, every community, every family should be a school of this spirituality. It requires the new evangelizer to experience deep conversion, a change of vision as well as conformity with the attitude and the mind of Christ, and communion with God. It requires a living faith in the Lord, the entrustment of oneself to God, a following of Jesus in mind, heart, and deed.

The "small flock" of Jesus should not be timid or fearful among Asia's billions, more than 60% of the world's population. For we have the singular resource of our faith, Jesus Christ himself, the unique gift of God to humanity. He journeys with us just as he did with his disciples on the way to Emmaus (*Luke* 24:13-32). At every Eucharistic celebration, he keeps opening our eyes and warming our hearts with the fire of love for a New Evangelization in Asia.

May Mary, the Mother of Jesus and our Mother, accompany us as we walk the roads of Asia, to "tell the story of Jesus." We are not to fear. We have the Lord's assurance, "Take heart, it is I; do not be afraid" (*Matthew* 14: 27). And we have his guarantee, "remember, I am with you always, to the end of the age" (*Matthew* 28:20).

THE FAITH-CULTURE DIALOGUE IN ASIA
Ten FABC Insights on Inculturation

The Federation of Asian Bishops' Conferences (FABC) has been a pivotal and influential body in the Asian Church since the Second Vatican Council. It has strengthened the bonds of communication among Catholic communities and their bishops and has contributed to the development of a shared vision of the Church and her evangelizing mission in Asia. The FABC asserts that the pathway for the Church in Asia to truly discover its own identity is to continually engage in a three-fold dialogue: with Asian peoples (especially the poor) [integral development], Asian cultures [inculturation], and Asian religions [interfaith dialogue]. This programmatic vision of a "triple dialogue" has constructively guided the FABC for over four decades. In a word, one can validly assert that the FABC is truly "Asia's Continuing Vatican II."

An FABC Introduction. Before addressing inculturation in Asia, the specific topic of this presentation, a brief background contextualization on the FABC appears necessary. The FABC is a transnational episcopal structure that brings together fourteen bishops' conferences from the following countries as full members: Bangladesh, India, Indonesia, Japan, Korea, Laos-Cambodia, Malaysia-Singapore-Brunei, Myanmar (Burma), Pakistan, Philippines, Sri Lanka, Taiwan, Thailand, and Vietnam. FABC has eleven associate members drawn from the ecclesiastical jurisdictions of East Timor, Hong Kong, Kazakhstan, Kyrgyzstan, Macau, Mongolia, Nepal, Siberia, Tadjikistan, Turkmenistan, and Uzbekistan. Thus, in total, twenty-eight countries are represented in the FABC, which grew out of the historic gathering of 180 Asian Catholic Bishops with Pope Paul VI during his 1970 Asian visit.

Aside from a modest central structure, there are nine FABC offices, which carry out many concrete initiatives and projects. The offices, purposely scattered among various Asian nations, are focused on evangelization, social communication, laity, human development, education and student chaplaincy, ecumenical and interreligious affairs, theological concerns, clergy, and consecrated life. Each of these offices sponsors a wide variety of activities that promote the growth of the Asian local Churches.

The supreme body of the FABC is the Plenary Assembly, which convenes approximately every four years. The themes, places, and dates of the ten plenary assemblies include the following: **I.** "Evangelization in Modern Day Asia" (Taipei, Taiwan: 1974); **II.** "Prayer—the Life of the Church in Asia" (Calcutta, India: 1978); **III.** "The Church—Community of Faith in Asia" (Bangkok, Thailand: 1982); **IV.** "The Vocation and Mission of the Laity in the Church and in the World of Asia" (Tokyo, Japan: 1986); **V.** "Journeying Together toward the Third Millennium" (Bandung, Indonesia: 1990); **VI.** "Christian Discipleship in Asia Today: Service to Life" (Manila, Philippines: 1995); **VII.** "A Renewed Church in Asia: A Mission of Love and Service" (Samphran, Thailand: 2000); **VIII.** "The Asian Family toward a Culture of Life" (Daejeon, Korea: 2004); **IX.** "Living the Eucharist in Asia" (Manila, Philippines: 2009); and, **X.** "FABC at Forty Years—Responding to the Challenges of Asia: New Evangelization" (Xuan Loc and Ho Chi Minh City, Vietnam: 2012).

The basic documents of the plenary assemblies and the initiatives of the FABC offices are available in the five volumes of *For All the Peoples of Asia* [*FAPA*] (Maryknoll, NY: Orbis Books and Quezon City, Philippines: Claretian Publications). The *FABC Papers*, continuously published since 1976, are available in print form and also in pdf format on the FABC website; see numbers 100 and 125 for comprehensive indexes. The five *FAPA* volumes and the individually numbered *FABC Papers* are indispensable resources for FABC material; both will be copiously utilized for this presentation. Thirty-four authors are cited in the selected bibliography; particularly apropos to the FABC and inculturation are the following: Bevans, FABC:TAC, Kroeger, Nemet, Phan, Tan, and Wilfred. To date (2014), over thirty doctoral dissertations have been completed on various FABC themes.

FABC Perspectives on Inculturation. The Asian local Churches are aware, enthusiastic, and committed to the pivotal challenge and obligation of inculturating the Christian faith in the Asian milieu, an assertion this presentation seeks to elaborate. "Asian" Church workers, both indigenous Asians as well as expatriate missionaries, view the inculturation of the Christian faith as a specific missionary and pastoral commitment.

An FABC statement, made over three decades ago, validly expresses their vision: "the decisive new phenomenon for Christianity in Asia will be the emergence of genuine Christian communities in Asia—Asian in their way of thinking, praying, living, communicating their own Christ-experience to others.... If the Asian Churches do not discover their own identity, they will have no future" (*FAPA I*, 70). This quote succinctly captures the urgent imperative of both building and strengthening each local Church to be, in the words of the First FABC Plenary Assembly in 1974, "a Church incarnate in a people, a Church indigenous and inculturated" (*FAPA I*, 14).

Capturing the FABC vision, extending over nearly four decades since its 1970 beginnings, may be a formidable task in a paper of modest length. This writer has chosen to identify ten pivotal "inculturation" themes as his approach to digesting the impressive body of FABC materials that are incredibly rich, amazingly visionary, and deeply inspirational. Each theme will be accorded a separate presentation, introduced by a short caption or title. In addition to the author's brief narrative, the FABC documents themselves will receive pride of place; pivotal quotes will form the bulk of the presentation, thus allowing the fresh, insightful vision of the FABC and the Asian Churches to emerge. Readers are encouraged to appreciate the spirit inherent in each of these ten themes and discover the action of the "befriending Spirit" at work fostering the emergence of genuine Asian Christian communities. This writer asserts that because the inculturating Asian Churches are discovering their own identity, they have a bright and hopeful future! The FABC continues to foster an "Asian Pentecost"!

I. An Urgent Imperative. A little known fact is that the word *inculturation* was used for the *first* time in Church parlance in Asia. When the Asian bishops met with Pope Paul VI in Manila in 1970, they reflected, as noted in their final statement, on "the inculturation of the life and message of the Gospel in Asia" (FAPA I, 6). Since that historic meeting from which the FABC eventually emerged, rooting the faith in Asian soil has remained a *leitmotif* of FABC concerns and reflection. The Christian communities of Asia continue to search for appropriate means to make the Church truly Catholic and truly Asian.

This struggle to integrate faith and life involves a process of ecclesial self-discovery. As noted above, Asians desire is to be "Asian in their way of thinking, praying, living, communicating their own Christ-experience to others," because they are convinced that if they "do not discover their own identity, they will have no future" (*FAPA I,* 70). It is imperative "to deepen the dialogue in Asia between the Gospel and culture, so that faith is inculturated and culture is evangelized" (*FAPA III,* 27). A constant refrain in FABC literature on evangelization is the desire for "intensifying our efforts, especially in the area of inculturation" (*FAPA III,* 215). One must also note that for the FABC the question of the faith-and-culture integration is primarily encountered *concretely and pastorally* as the local Churches engage with people and all the life-realities of Asia.

For Asian Christians, this is an *urgent imperative* due to the perceived "foreignness" of the Church. A 1991 FABC theological consultation stated the challenge quite starkly: "As a social institution the Church is perceived as a foreign body in its colonial origins while other world religions are not. The lingering colonial image survives.... The Church is even sometimes seen as an obstacle or threat to national integration and religious and cultural identity.... The Church remains foreign in its lifestyle, in its institutional structure, in its worship, in its western trained leadership and in its theology. Christian rituals often remain formal, neither spontaneous nor particularly Asian.... Seminary formation often alienates the seminarian from the people. Biblical, systematic and historical theology as taught are often unpastoral and unAsian" (*FAPA II*, 195-196).

While honestly admitting the enormity of the challenge, Asian Christians do see significant opportunities emerging. "As Asia comes out of the colonial period, its people have become more aware of their national identity. There is a renewed sense of pride in their religious and cultural values.... Reviewing the life of the Church in Asia since Vatican II, we find that the Churches in Asia recognize the indispensable necessity of inculturation as a path of mission. This has been constantly reiterated by the official documents of FABC and the National Episcopal Conferences.... The emergence of indigenous theology, spirituality, religious life, creativity in liturgical celebrations, etc. are clear evidence of the commitment the Churches have made to achieve this goal [inculturated evangelization]" (*FAPA III*, 217). Yet, the urgency of the imperative remains.

II. A Descriptive Definition. One looks in vain in the FABC literature to find a consistent definition of culture and inculturation. For example, in the early FABC documents, terms like "adaptation," "incarnation," "acculturation," "indigenization," and "inculturation" were often used interchangeably. Yet, this lack of a single term has resulted in a wide variety of descriptions of the inculturation process, some of which boarder on the poetic. While maybe not sociologically or theologically precise, these various descriptions elicit a vision or dream of the mission to be accomplished.

In 1970 the Asian bishops committed themselves to "develop an indigenous theology and to do what we can so that the life and meaning of the Gospel may be ever more incarnate in the rich historical cultures of Asia, so that ... Asian Christianity may help promote all that is 'authentically human in these cultures'" (*FAPA I*, 9). The 1974 FABC plenary assembly states: "Indigenization renders the local church truly present within the life and cultures of our peoples. Through it, all their human reality is assumed into the life of the Body of Christ, so that all of it may be purified and healed, perfected and fulfilled"; the same assembly listed several key tasks in the preaching the Gospel in Asia, one of which is "*Inculturation*, which renders the local church present within the life of our people" (*FAPA I*, 16, 23).

The 1979 mission conference in Manila devoted one workshop precisely to inculturation as an Asian missionary task. Precious insights were forthcoming. "Inculturation is not mere adaptation of a ready-made Christianity into a given situation, but rather a creative embodiment of the Word in the local church. This is the basic and fundamental process of inculturation.... In this process of inculturation a people receives the Word, makes it the principle of their life, values, attitudes and aspirations. In this way they become the Body of Christ in this particular time and place—a local church.... The community discovers a new identity, losing nothing of its cultural riches, but integrating them in a new whole and becoming the sacrament of God's liberating love active among men" (*FAPA I*, 138).

As the FABC vision of inculturation matured over the years, an earlier "uni-directional" view [from faith into culture] is clearly replaced by a dialogical understanding. "Inculturation is a dialogical encounter process understood in its deepest meaning that comes from the salvific movement of the Triune God, because evangelization itself is above all a dialogue between the Gospel message and the given reality" (*FAPA I*, 138-139).

The "Theses on the Local Church" by the FABC Theological Advisory Commission notes that mutuality and reciprocity are essential to inculturation. Thus, an inculturated Church "comes into existence and is built up through a deep and mutually enriching encounter between the Gospel and a people with its particular culture and tradition.... Inculturation consists not only in the expression of the Gospel and the Christian faith through the cultural medium, but includes, as well, experiencing, understanding and appropriating them through the cultural resources of a people. As a result, the concrete shape of the local church will be, on the one hand, conditioned by the culture, and, on the other hand, the culture will be evangelized by the life and witness of the local Church" (*FABC Papers 60*, 18).

A comprehensive analysis of the copious FABC material shows that through time and experience an integral view of culture and inculturation emerges. Both elements are to be understood in a holistic sense; they incorporate "all the life-realities" of a given people; they encompass "whatever truly belongs to that people: its meanings and its values, its aspirations, its thought and its language, its songs and its artistry—even its frailties and failings its assumes, so that they too may be healed" (*FAPA I*, 14). Because culture is dynamic, inculturation will address "the emergent cultures of Asia, a combination of many diverse elements of modern civilization, yet still rooted in local traditional values" (*FAPA II*, 198). In the FABC perspective, the dynamic presence of the Holy Spirit is imperative, given the complexity of culture and the challenge of inculturation (*FAPA I*, 73, 130).

III. A Dialogical Approach. The FABC is eminently clear in stating its conviction about what approach is needed for rooting the faith in Asia. "Dialogue is a primary means and way for *inculturation*" (*FAPA I*, 142). "We perceive dialogue as a necessary condition and instrument for *inculturation*" (*FAPA I*, 249). These assertions are consistent with the FABC's comprehensive view of mission and evangelization. "Mission may find its greatest urgency in Asia; it also finds in our continent a distinctive mode [dialogue].... Mission in Asia will also seek through *dialogue* to serve the cause of unity of the peoples of Asia marked by such a diversity of beliefs, cultures, and socio-political structures" (*FAPA I*, 281-282). "The local Churches of Asia will proclaim Jesus Christ to their fellow humans in a dialogical manner" (*FAPA I*, 346).

A dialogical approach is the only possible avenue, given the multiracial, multilinguistic, multireligious, and multicultural reality of Asia, the earth's largest continent and home to nearly two-thirds of the world's population. Such a dialogical approach is not a mere external methodology that the Church in Asia will adapt; the Church herself is called to be "a community of dialogue. This dialogical model is in fact a new way of being Church" (*FAPA I*, 332).

As a community of dialogue, the local Church "is never centered on itself but on the coming true of God's dream for the world" (*FAPA I*, 333). Such an engaged Church "will necessarily be transformed in the process. In other words, it will become inculturated—at a level which includes but goes deeper than changes in ritual and symbol. Such a Church may at last become a Church of Asia and not simply a Church in Asia. It may then be perceived as no longer an alien presence. In this model of Church, dialogue, liberation, inculturation and proclamation are but different aspects of the one reality" (*FAPA I*, 333).

The dialogical approach finds its roots in the earliest FABC sources. The programmatic document "Evangelization in Modern Day Asia" from the First FABC Plenary Assembly in 1974 outlined a unique kind of dialogue; it noted that building up a truly local Church, one that is "indigenous and inculturated," demands a faith-community that is in "continuous, humble and loving dialogue with the living traditions, the cultures, the religions—in brief, with all the life-realities of the people in whose midst it has sunk its roots deeply and whose history and life it gladly makes its own" (*FAPA I*, 14).

This "triple dialogue" paradigm has been verified in subsequent FABC assemblies; the Seventh FABC Plenary

Assembly in 2000 noted that the "triple dialogue" that the FABC developed "over the past thirty years ... is still valid today" (*FAPA III*, 4). The dialogue approach revolves around three key poles: local Church, dialogue, and the Asian peoples and their realities. Almost simplistically, it can be represented in a schema (presented in an earlier chapter):

		ASIA'S PEOPLE (POOR)
LOCAL CHURCH	**<< DIALOGUE >>**	**ASIA'S CULTURES**
(subject)	(approach)	**ASIA'S RELIGIONS**

One must point out that the arrows on either side of the word *dialogue* move in two directions. Certainly, this indicates that this dialogical approach is always a two-fold process of dynamic interaction. There is always mutual reinforcement; this means that while the Church influences the people, their cultures and religions, the Church herself is concomitantly being shaped and molded. In a word, the dynamic of inculturation is always at work.

This *operative paradigm* of holistic evangelization [the "triple dialogue" approach] is the *interpretive key* to understanding and appreciating the inculturation process in Asia today. This is how the Church "lives and breathes" in Asia. Here one finds the Holy Spirit at work. This is an authentic reception and continuation of the Second Vatican Council in Asia.

IV. Primary Actor: Local Church. Explore any major document that has emerged from the extensive reflection of the FABC and you will probably find several creative insights on the local Church in the Asian context. It was the 1970 Asian pastoral visit of Pope Paul VI with the Asian bishops that gave the impetus for the local Churches to begin formulating a vision of Church and mission adequate to the "new world being born" in Asia in the post-colonial period. They asked themselves: How would the Churches incarnate a decisive "turning to history" and a "turning to the Gospel" within history "for all the peoples of Asia"? How would the FABC articulate an overall vision that captures what "being Church in Asia today" truly means. This is the context for appreciating the role of the local Church in the inculturation process.

The Fifth FABC Plenary Assembly held in Indonesia in 1990 added new clarity and focus by asserting that it is the local Church which is "the acting subject of mission." The final document stated: "The renewal of our sense of mission will mean … that the acting subject of mission is the *local Church* living and acting in communion with the universal Church. It is the local Churches and communities which can discern and work out (in dialogue with each other and with other persons of goodwill) the way the Gospel is best proclaimed, the Church set up, the values of God's Kingdom realized in their own place and time" (*FAPA I*, 281).

The statement continues: "In fact, it is by responding to and serving the needs of the peoples of Asia that the different Christian communities become truly local Churches. This local Church, which is the acting subject of mission, is the people of God in a given milieu, the whole Christian community—laity, Religious and clergy. It is the whole diocese, the parish, the Basic Ecclesial Community and other groups. Their time has come for Asia" (*FAPA I*, 281).

As the FABC asserts that the local Church is the "acting subject of mission," it concomitantly affirms that it is the "acting subject of inculturation," since inculturation is essential in contemporary mission. In addition, since the local Church is the *entire* people of God, the inculturation process demands the involvement of *all* members of the Christian community. Authentic inculturation presumes—even demands—a fully participative Christian community.

The FABC corpus is rich with statements affirming the pivotal role of the local Church in inculturation. "Dialogue with cultures or inculturation takes place when the local Church lives its faith and the Gospel in terms of the cultures of its peoples, the Church being enriched internally by these cultures and in turn transforming them from within" (*FAPA I*, 266). "Local Churches, servant and inculturated, are the subject of the evangelizing mission" (*FAPA II*, 202). As a living cell of the local Church, the Basic Ecclesial Community or Small Christian Community is to serve as "a seedbed of inculturation" (*FAPA III*, 110).

In the FABC perspective, becoming truly local Churches, an urgent task in Asia today, demands that "more and more the local Churches in Asia must see themselves as responsible agents for the self-realization of the Church.... We grasp something of the significance of local Church and inculturation in this context; those who cannot understand this fail to resonate with the signs of our time, and the heartbeat of our peoples" (*FABC Papers 60*, 52).

"Asian Churches then must become truly Asian in all things. The principle of indigenization and inculturation is at the very root of their coming into their own. The ministry of Asian Churches, if it is to be authentic, must be relevant to Asian societies. This calls on the part of the Churches for originality, creativity and inventiveness, for boldness and courage" (*FAPA I*, 72-73). Indeed, "if the Asian Churches do not discover their own identity, they will have no future" (*FAPA I*, 70).

V. An Interfaith Linkage. A previous section of this presentation was devoted to the dialogical approach essential to inculturation in the Asian context. It spoke about FABC's "triple dialogue" paradigm and noted that the Asian religions are one of the key "dialogue partners" of the local Church. Building upon that previous discussion, this section turns to the place of Asia's venerable religions in the inculturation process.

Eighty-five percent of all the world's followers of other living faiths (besides Christianity) are Asians. Christians in Asia are less than three percent of the total population. In short, except for the Philippines and East Timor, Christians are a small minority. There are seven times more Muslims in Asia than there are Christians; the four largest Islamic countries in the world (2007 statistics) are in Asia: Indonesia (216 million), Pakistan (161 million), India (147 million), Bangladesh (122 million). These brief Islamic statistical facts (not to mention Buddhism and Hinduism) are concrete realities confronting the Church, her vision and praxis.

The FABC is very aware of the challenge posed by these demographics. In addition, there is "a strong interrelation in Asia between religion and culture" and often "Asia tends to identify nationality, religion and culture" (*FAPA II*, 194). "Religion, providing ... contact of the human with the Divine, is the soul of culture" (*FAPA II*, 21). "Each culture provides the context for understanding reality and expressing religious faith" (*FAPA II*, 23). A pivotal question surfaces: How does the FABC view these Asian religions vis-à-vis inculturation?

In brief, the FABC takes a positive approach to the religions, promoting constructive collaboration, dialogue, and critical interaction. The presence of the "seeds of the Word" and the action of the Holy Spirit in these religions is affirmed. Thus, they have insights, values, and virtues that can inform the Church's inculturation process. No detailing of the numerous FABC interfaith workshops and activities is possible or necessary; it is sufficient to sensitively listen to the FABC perspectives, perceiving how they can positively influence an in-depth inculturation.

The First Plenary Assembly in 1974 gave this orientation toward the religions in its final statement—expressed with poetic elegance. It asserts that building up a truly local Church "involves a dialogue with the great religious traditions of our peoples. In this dialogue we accept them as significant and positive elements in the economy of God's design of salvation. In them we recognize and respect profound spiritual and ethical meanings and values. Over many centuries they have been the treasury of the religious experience of our ancestors, from which our contemporaries do not cease to draw light and strength. They have been (and continue to be) the authentic expression of the noblest longings of their hearts, and the home of their contemplation and prayer. They have helped to give shape to the histories and cultures of our nations" (*FAPA I*, 14).

Springing from this positive assessment, the bishops continue: "How then can we not give them reverence and honor? And how can we not acknowledge that God has drawn our peoples to Himself through them? Only in dialogue with these religions can we discover in them the seeds of the Word of God (*Ad Gentes*, c. I, 9). This dialogue will allow us to touch the expression and the reality of our peoples' deepest selves, and enable us to find authentic ways of living and expressing our own Christian faith. It will reveal to us also many riches of our own faith which we perhaps would not have perceived. Thus it can become a sharing in friendship of our quest for God and for brotherhood among His sons. Finally, this dialogue will teach us what our faith in Christ leads us to receive from these religious traditions, and what must be purified in them, healed and made whole, in the light of God's Word" (FABC I, 14-15).

Dialogue with Asia's religious traditions is also an occasion to give witness to Christian faith: "On our part we can offer what we believe the Church alone has the duty and joy to offer to them and to all men: oneness with the Father in Jesus His Son, the ways to grace Christ gives us in His Gospel and His sacraments, and fellowship [in] the community which seeks to live in Him; an understanding too of the value of the human person and of the social dimensions of human salvation" (FABC I, 15). Indeed, this is a wonderfully balanced assessment of Asia's religions—and a clear rationale for involving them in the Church's efforts to foster inculturation.

VI. An Asian Pastoral Method. As noted earlier, in Asia the "faith-and-culture integration" is primarily encountered *concretely and pastorally*, rather than theoretically or theologically; this reality is reflected in the FABC documents themselves. It also has another ramification related to the pastoral methodology promoted by the FABC. To facilitate the growth of an inculturated local Church, the FABC has evolved a unique approach of pastoral engagement. This four-stage "Asian" methodology has been termed: the "Pastoral Spiral" (cf. *FAPA I*, 231-232).

The process begins with *exposure-immersion*; it may also be called "entering into a dialogue-of-life." Exposure-Immersion follows the basic principle of the Incarnation; local Christians seek to share the daily lives of their neighbors and communities. They seek to understand and appreciate—through direct experience and interaction—the life situation shared by Muslims, Buddhists, Hindus, and Christians. In a word, all are invited to practice "good neighbor-ology."

The second stage of *social analysis* follows. Communities try to evaluate the social, economic, political, cultural, and religious systems in society. They observe and analyze events and trends, discerning the impact of rapid social change on human lives. They evaluate the signs of contemporary times, the events of history, as well as the needs and aspirations of people and communities. It is an interfaith effort to comprehend the realities that shape their lives.

Asians have seen the necessity of integrating social analysis (stage two) with the *contemplative dimension* (stage three) of integral evangelization; this third stage of faith reflection emerges from Asia's religio-cultural heritage. Through this contemplation people discover God's presence and activity within social realities, discerning not only negative and enslaving social aspects, but also the positive, prophetic aspects of life that can inspire genuine God-awareness and spirituality. This stage in the total process has proven very beneficial; for example, it enables the poor to make their unique contribution to inculturation; it brings prayer and spirituality into the endeavor.

The third stage of ongoing spiritual-theological reflection issues into the fourth stage called *pastoral planning*, which seeks to translate the previous three stages into actual, realizable mission plans of action. Indeed, concrete, inculturated programs of evangelization are ultimately necessary, but they are better conceived through this Asian process that actively discerns what the Lord of history is challenging the Church to be and to do.

One should note that this process is a *spiral*—it must be repeated frequently; hopefully, at each turn or cycle it moves upward and forward. The FABC, committed to this approach of inculturated evangelization, has further developed it through numerous AsIPA programs [As = Asian, I = Integral, P = Pastoral, A = Approach] (cf. *FAPA II*, 107-111; *FAPA III*, 107-112). These initiatives concretely respond to the criticism: "At times our efforts towards inculturation have remained too theoretical and failed to resonate with the people at the grass-roots level" (*FAPA III*, 216).

A final, brief "footnote" may be added to link the FABC pastoral spiral and AsIPA programs with the "see, judge, act" methodology, traditionally associated with programs of Catholic Action. This approach to social transformation encourages Christians to "see" (observe concrete social realities), "judge" (analyze and evaluate these realities), and "act" (make decisions and take concrete steps to transform the reality). FABC has enunciated a similar approach, expressed with the "3-D" terminology; Asian Churches must "dialogue" with life's realities, then prayerfully "discern" the situation in faith, and lastly, engage in appropriate Christ-like "deeds" to transform the situation (cf. *FAPA I*, 281-285). There are, ultimately, many parallels in these inductive pastoral approaches (whatever one names them); the crucial factor is that the Christian community, motivated by Gospel faith and anchored in concrete life situations, remains actively engaged in the transformation of the world. The result is true inculturation, the result of faith-filled praxis.

VII. Pastoral Concerns and Ministries. FABC pastoral-theological reflection is decidedly inductive—emerging from life's concrete realities. Consequently, many FABC documents frequently identify specific pastoral concerns, because the

Church seeks to be—in fact, not only in theory—the "Church of the poor" and the "Church of the young"; she shares the vicissitudes of the "Church of silence" in several parts of Asia (cf. *FAPA I*, 5-6, 18). Her pastoral priorities concern the displaced (refugees and migrants), women and the girl-child, youth, workers, families, the indigenous peoples, etc. (cf. *FAPA III*, 9-11). As the Church addresses these specific concerns, she tries to develop a theology and praxis which will be "a service to life"; she "initiates and develops a process of inculturation" (*FAPA II*, 226-227).

Considering the numerous areas of pastoral concern that beckon the Asian Church's compassionate involvement, the FABC organized the highly successful 1977 Asian Colloquium on Ministries in the Church [ACMC] (*FAPA I*, 67-92). The FABC noted the intimate link between pastoral concerns and the necessary ministries to meet these same concerns. Thus, the ACMC investigated "the theological context and the experiential reality of the Church's ministries"; it focused on the "endeavor to make the ministries of our Churches more relevant to our times and better suited to meet the needs of our peoples" (*FAPA I*, 67-68).

The colloquium proceeded with the awareness that each local Church as she is led by her servant Lord "has to discover time and again what ministries and what ministerial structures she requires in order to fulfill her mission to offer to a human society the salvation brought about by Jesus Christ" (*FAPA I*, 72). In a word, the ACMC was about developing "inculturated ministries." The gathering strongly affirmed that "Asian Churches then must become truly Asian in all things" (*FAPA I*, 72)—including her ministries and ministerial structures.

The ACMC was not about getting additional workers for Church apostolates; its focus was development of "appropriate" ministries, inculturated ministries. The ACMC noted: "The servant Church can never adequately exercise her ministeriality through one uniform type of ministry"; the Church accomplishes mission "by creating new forms of ministries, alongside the existing ones…. The exact form of these ministries will depend to a great extent on the local situations in our countries" (*FAPA I*, 78).

A 1988 FABC assembly noted: "Inculturation appears to us as indispensable to prepare Christian communities and their leaders for dialogue…. Hence we suggest that the process of inculturation in our Christian communities be deepened and that the formators (pastors, seminary professors, catechists, community organizers) be given specific training in inculturation…" (*FAPA I*, 311). The process of fostering inculturated ministries in Asia remains an ongoing FABC commitment.

VIII. Links with Spirituality. The Second FABC Plenary Assembly in 1978 focused on "Prayer—The Life of the Church of Asia"; it was held in Calcutta, India, the land of prayer and pilgrimage centers where the Christian ashram movement has flourished in recent years. The final 1978 statement is a rich resource for appreciating how the Church can both give and receive from the spiritual treasury of Asia's venerable religions. This is a fertile ground for inculturation.

Asia's bishops noted: "In keeping with the economy of the Incarnation…, the prayer-life of our local Churches should 'take over the riches of our nations, which have been given to Christ as inheritance.' Important above all, in our present context, are those ways of prayer which have been developed by the native genius of our peoples…. We are daily more convinced that the Spirit is leading us in our time, not to some dubious syncretism (which we all rightly reject), but to an integration—profound and organic in character—of all that is best in our traditional ways of prayer and worship, into the treasury of our Christian heritage" (*FAPA I*, 34-35).

"Asia has much to give to authentic Christian spirituality: a richly developed prayer of the whole person in unity of body-psyche-spirit; prayer of deep interiority and immanence; traditions of asceticism and renunciation; techniques of contemplation found in the ancient eastern religions; simplified prayer-forms and other popular expressions of faith and piety of those whose hearts and minds so readily turn to God in their daily lives. This is Asia's gift of prayer to the Church" (*FAPA I*, 42).

The FABC Theological Advisory Commission has also shown the "inculturation potential" of Asia's religions. They write: "The life in the Spirit, which is spirituality, must be attuned to and reflect the experience of the Spirit by a people in their culture and tradition. For we know that the Spirit is present and active among peoples of Asia, in their histories, traditions, cultures and religions. *Inculturation will be thus a meeting of the Spirit with the Spirit,* fostering the bonds of spiritual communion and solidarity with the people among whom the local Church lives and grows [emphasis added]. The spiritual riches and religious values by which the people of our continent have been nourished through millennia and centuries must flow into the life of the local Church to enrich it" (*FABC Papers 60*, 29).

IX. The "Asian Way" of Being Church. The Fifth FABC Plenary Assembly in Indonesia used a phrase that has captured the imagination of many Asian Christians; the bishops' final statement speaks about "a new way of being Church." The phrase is meant to envision "alternate ways of being Church in the Asia of the 1990s." Several key dimensions of this "new" community were noted: the Church is to be "a communion of communities," a "participatory Church," a "prophetic sign," a "Spirit-filled community" (*FAPA I*, 287-288).

For some unfamiliar with the growth of the local Churches in Asia after Vatican II, the phrase "new way of being Church" may raise questions. The phrase implies no rejection of essential dimensions of ecclesiology; it attempts to capture the aspirations of Asian Christians to live their faith in the Christian community in an "Asian way." This "new way of being Church ... is nothing more and nothing less than a following of Jesus-in-mission, an authentic discipleship in the context of

Asia.... For the spirituality of the new way of being Church is the spirituality of those who place their complete trust in the Lord." Their lives are marked by "Gospel values [that] resonate deeply with the cultures of Asia" (*FAPA I*, 288). In a word, the phrase expresses well the deep desire to be an inculturated Christian community.

Building on the Fifth FABC Plenary Assembly and its vision of "a new way of being Church," the Seventh FABC Plenary Assembly in 2000 spoke about "the challenge of discerning the Asian way." While noting that "Asia is a cultural mosaic shining with its rich diversity," Asia's bishops stated their position: "We are committed to the emergence of the Asianness of the Church in Asia. This means that the Church has to be an embodiment of the Asian vision and values of life, especially interiority, harmony, a holistic and inclusive approach to every area of life" (*FAPA III*, 8).

The bishops noted: "For thirty years [since the founding of the FABC in 1970], as we have tried to reformulate our Christian identity in Asia, we have addressed different issues, one after another.... These issues are not separate topics to be discussed, but aspects of an integrated approach to our Mission of Love and Service. We need to feel and act 'integrally'.... Inculturation, dialogue, justice, and the option for the poor are aspects of whatever we do." Rejoicing in the "Asian Way" of being Church and seeing it as a gift of the Spirit, the bishops stated: "We are aware that this Asianness, founded on solid values, is a special gift the world is waiting" (*FAPA III*, 8-9). This is Asia's gift to the entire Church.

X. Special Themes—Not to be Lost. This final section is, in fact, a kind of potpourri of many smaller insights on inculturation from the FABC perspective. One will not find a detailed "theology of inculturation" in the FABC material, which is decidedly pastoral in its orientation. However, solid theological underpinnings are found in several FABC documents. Some brief "theological roots" are noted.

The Church as a pilgrim in history "needs to be conformed to Jesus and his Reign, lest the quality of her witness be impaired.... The same conformity of the Church to her master is the decisive theological foundation for the inculturation of the local Churches" (*FAPA II*, 201); in a particular way, this is related to the theology of the Incarnation (*FAPA I*, 14, 34, 46).

In several places the FABC notes that inculturation will follow the pattern of the paschal mystery. "This Paschal Mystery thus constitutes the law and meaning of the life and mission of the Church. The process of incarnation/inculturation thus calls for the process of death and resurrection, so that the Church, and the local Church in its own time and place, may become truly the sign and instrument ... [of] the Crucified and Risen Lord" (*FABC Papers 60*, 34). FABC notes the process of inculturation: "This necessary but painful and complex process is the cross and resurrection of inculturation" (*FAPA I*, 150-151); it also "demands a *kenosis* modeled after that of Jesus [and] ... *Kenosis* implies death and resurrection" (*FAPA I*, 331).

Several additional themes related to inculturation surface in the FABC corpus of documents. One finds an emphasis on the theology of harmony (*FAPA I*, 249, 317-322; *FAPA II*, 163-164, 229-298). Special care must be taken to preserve the cultures of Asia's many indigenous peoples (*FAPA III*, 227-229). The Church appreciates her task of promoting a culture of integral life (*FAPA IV*, 18) and the challenge to evangelize culture (*FAPA IV*, 33-34). The "faith-culture" dynamic should receive special attention by the Church (*FAPA III*, 28-29). Other FABC topics relevant to inculturation could be noted; those mentioned here suffice to emphasize the continuing role of Asia's dynamic Churches in the whole inculturation process.

Conclusion. This presentation has focused on the dialogue of faith and culture in Asia; it has surfaced ten thematic insights of the FABC. In this endeavor, the journey of the Churches in Asia to become "truly local Churches" and "truly Asian in all things" has emerged; they struggle to enflesh "a new way of being Church" in the Asia of the third millennium.

This journey of four decades, since the beginnings of the FABC in 1970, has been perceptively described in the final document of the Seventh FABC Plenary Assembly in 2000. The "call of the Spirit to the local Churches in Asia ... to be truly inculturated local Churches" can be understood as "a concerted series of movements toward a renewed Church," captured in eight overarching movements.

The FABC sees its growth as: (1) a movement towards a Church of the Poor and a Church of the Young; (2) a movement toward a "truly local Church," toward a Church "incarnate in a people, a Church indigenous and inculturated"; (3) a movement toward deep interiority and a praying community; (4) a movement toward an authentic community of faith; (5) a movement toward active integral evangelization, toward a new sense of mission; (6) a movement toward empowerment of men and women; (7) a movement toward the service of life in Asia; and, (8) a movement toward the triple dialogue with other faiths, with the poor, and with Asian cultures (cf. *FAPA III*, 2-4).

This eight-fold movement of growth of the local Churches in the FABC region of Asia, particularly in the Vatican II era, is indeed: "Good News from Asia." It is an inspiring story of faith and service. It is a profound witness to the action of the befriending Spirit in Asia. It is a story of a Church renewed in its evangelizing mission. It is a narrative of God's love becoming incarnate, a story of inculturation.

FABC PERSPECTIVES ON INCULTURATION
A Selected Bibliography

Amaladoss, M. **(A)** "Culture and Dialogue," *Vidyajyoti* 49:1 (1985): 6-15; **(B)** "Inculturation and Ignatian Spirituality," *Way Supplement* 79 (1994): 39-47.

Amalorpavadass, D. "Gospel and Culture: Evangelisation and Inculturation," *FABC Papers 15*. Hong Kong: FABC Secretariat, 1979: 1-51.

Arévalo, C. G. "Prenotes to the Contextualization of Theology," *Philippiniana Sacra* 14:40 (1979): 15-35.

Bevans, S. "Inculturation of Theology in Asia: The Federation of Asian Bishops' Conferences, 1970-1995," *Studia Missionalia* 45 (1996): 1-23; see also: *FABC Papers 78*. Hong Kong: FABC Secretariat, 1997: 20-36.

Cajilig, V. (Ed.). *Dialogue between Faith and Culture.* Manila: FABC Office of Education and Student Chaplaincy, 1998.

Chia, E. (A) (Ed.). *Dialogue: Resource Manual for Catholics in Asia.* Bangkok: FABC Office of Ecumenical and Interreligious Affairs, 2001; **(B)** "Thirty Years of FABC: History, Foundation, Context and Theology," *FABC Papers 106*. Hong Kong: FABC Secretariat, 2003: 1-55.

Chupungco, A. (A) *Cultural Adaptation of the Liturgy.* New York: Paulist Press, 1982; **(B)** *Liturgies of the Future: The Process and Methods of Inculturation.* New York: Paulist Press, 1989; **(C)** *Liturgical Inculturation: Sacramentals, Religiosity, and Catechesis.* Collegeville: Liturgical Press, 1992; **(D)** "*Liturgiam Authenticam* and Inculturation," *East Asian Pastoral Review* 39:1 (2002): 95-100.

Claver, F. "Inculturation as Dialogue," in: **Phan, P.** (Ed.). *The Asian Synod.* Maryknoll, NY: Orbis Books, 2002: 100-102.

De Mesa, J. "Doing Theology as Inculturation in the Asian Context," in: **Scherer, J.** and **Bevans, S.** (Eds.). *New Directions in Mission and Evangelization 3.* Maryknoll, NY: Orbis Books, 1999: 117-133.

Dhavamony, M. (A) (Ed.). *Inculturation* [*Studia Missionalia* 44]. Rome: Editrice Pontificia Università

Gregoriana, 1995; **(B)** *Christian Theology of Inculturation.* Rome: Editrice Pontificia Università Gregoriana, 1997.

Dinh Duc Dao, J. "Evangelization and Culture in Asia: Problems and Prospects," *Omnis Terra* 28:245 (1994): 70-80.

Divarkar, P. *et al.* "The Encounter of the Gospel with Culture," *FABC Papers* 7. Hong Kong: FABC Secretariat, 1978: 1-36.

Dias, M., Kroeger, J., Perera, J., Prior, J., and **Saldanha, J.** (Eds.). *Rooting Faith in Asia: Source Book for Inculturation.* Bangalore, India and Quezon City, Philippines: Claretian Publications, 2005.

Dupuis, J. "FABC Focus on the Church's Evangelising Mission in Asia Today," *Vidyajyoti* 56:9 (1992): 449-468.

Eilers, F-J. [**Rosales, G., Arévalo, C.G.,** and **Tirimanna, V.**] (Eds.). *For All the Peoples of Asia I-II-III-IV-V* [five volumes of FABC Documents]. Maryknoll, NY: Orbis Books and Quezon City, Philippines: Claretian Publications, 1992, 1997, 2002, 2007, and 2014. Common abbreviation: *FAPA.*

FABC:TAC (Federation of Asian Bishops' Conferences: Theological Advisory Commission). "Theses on the Local Church" (see theses 5-12 on inculturation), in: **Gnanapiragasam, J.** and **Wilfred, F.** (Eds.). *Being Church in Asia.* Quezon City, Philippines: Claretian Publications, 1994: 33-89; available also as *FABC Papers 60.* Hong Kong: FABC Secretariat, 1991: 1-58.

Hardawiryana, R. "Building the Church of Christ in a Pluralistic Situation: A Pastoral Primer on Christian Inculturation," *FABC Papers 41.* Hong Kong: FABC Secretariat, 1985: 1-35; also published: Rome: Pontifical Gregorian University, 1986.

Ko, M. "Evangelization as Inculturation as Seen in *Ecclesia in Asia*," in: **Dias, M.** (Ed.) *Evangelization in the Light of*

Ecclesia in Asia. Bangalore: Claretian Publications, 2003: 188-209.

Kroeger, J. **(A)** "FABC Papers Comprehensive Index (1976-2001)," *FABC Papers 100*. Hong Kong: FABC Secretariat, 2001: 1-58; an expanded version is found in *FAPA IV* (2007), Appendix II; **(B)** Edited with **P. Phan.** *The Future of the Asian Churches: The Asian Synod and Ecclesia in Asia*. Quezon City, Philippines: Claretian Publications, 2002; **(C)** *Becoming Local Church*. Quezon City, Philippines: Claretian Publications, 2003; **(D)** "Asia's Dynamic, Missionary Local Churches: FABC Perspectives," *Landas* (Manila) 19:2 (2005): 175-207; **(E)** "Inculturation in Asia – *Quo Vadis?" Philippiniana Sacra* 41:122 (2006): 237-332; similar publication: "Inculturation in Asia: Directions, Initiatives, and Options," *FABC Papers 115*. Hong Kong: FABC Secretariat, 2005: 1-117; **(F)** "FABC Papers Comprehensive Index (2001-2008)," *FABC Papers 125*. Hong Kong: FABC Secretariat, 2008: 1-48; a similar version is found in *FAPA V* (2014), Special Appendix, 1-48.

Lambino, A. "Inculturation in Asia: Going beyond First Gear," *Landas* 1 (1987): 72-80.

Legrand, L. *The Bible on Culture*. Maryknoll, NY: Orbis Books, 2000.

Menamparampil, T. *The Challenge of Cultures*. Bombay: St. Pauls, 1996.

Nemet, L. "Inculturation in the FABC Documents," *East Asian Pastoral Review* 31:1-2 (1994): 77-94.

Nguyen Nhu, S. "Inculturation in the Context of the Veneration of Ancestors," in: Phan, P. (Ed.). *The Asian Synod*. Maryknoll, NY: Orbis Books, 2002: 124-126.

Phan, P. **(A)** *Christianity with an Asian Face*. Maryknoll, NY: Orbis Books, 2003; **(B)** *In Our Own Tongues: Perspectives from Asia on Mission and Inculturation*. Maryknoll, NY: Orbis

Books, 2003; **(C)** *Being Religious Interreligiously*. Maryknoll, NY: Orbis Books, 2004; **(D)** "Cultural Diversity and Religious Pluralism: The Church's Mission in Asia," *East Asian Pastoral Review* 43:2 (2006): 109-128.

Pieris, A. (A) "Inculturation: Some Critical Reflections," *Vidyajyoti* 57:11 (1993): 641-651; **(B)** "Inculturation in Asia: A Theological Reflection on an Experience," in: *Yearbook of Contextual Theologies*. Frankfurt: Interkulturelle Kommunikation, 1994: 59-71.

Prior, J. "Dignity and Identity: The Struggle of Indigenous Peoples in Asia to Preserve, Purify and Promote their Cultures," *FABC Papers 104*. Hong Kong: FABC Secretariat, 2002: 1-34.

Roest Crollius, A. (A) "What is so New about Inculturation?" *Gregorianum* 59:4 (1978): 721-738; **(B)** "Sense and Nonsense about Inculturation," *Sevartham* 20 (1995): 3-12; **(C)** "Inculturation in Asia and *Ecclesia in Asia*," in: **Kroeger, J.** and **Phan, P.** (Eds.). *The Future of the Asian Churches: The Asian Synod and Ecclesia in Asia*. Quezon City, Philippines: Claretian Publications, 2002: 102-109.

Rogers, A. (Ed.). *Colloquium on Church in Asia in the 21st Century*. Manila: FABC Office for Human Development, 1997.

Saldanha, J. *Inculturation*. Bandra, India: St. Pauls, 1996.

Standaert, N. *Inculturation: The Gospel and Cultures*. Pasay City, Philippines: Saint Paul Publications, 1990.

Tan, J. (A) "Constructing an Asian Theology of Liturgical Inculturation from the Documents of the Federation of Asian Bishops' Conferences (FABC)," *East Asian Pastoral Review* 36:4 (1999): 383-401; parallel presentation found in: *FABC Papers 89*. Hong Kong: FABC Secretariat, 1999: 1-60; **(B)** "Theologizing at the Service of Life: The Contextual Theological Methodology of the FABC," *Gregorianum* 81:3 (2000): 541-

575; see also: *FABC Papers 108*. Hong Kong: FABC Secretariat, 2003: 1-34; **(C)** *"Missio Inter Gentes*: Towards a New Paradigm in the Mission Theology of the FABC," *FABC Papers 109*. Hong Kong: FABC Secretariat, 2004: 1-38.

Tesoro, D. and **Jose, J.** (Eds.). *The Rise of Filipino Theology*. Pasay City, Philippines: Paulines, 2004.

Wilfred, F. (A) "Inculturation as a Hermeneutical Question," *Vidyajyoti* 52:9 (1988): 422-436; **(B)** "Fifth Plenary Assembly of FABC: An Interpretation of its Theological Orientation," *Vidyajyoti* 54:11 (1990): 583-592; **(C)** "What the Spirit Says to the Churches (Rev. 2:7): A FABC Vademecum," *Vidyajyoti* 62:2 (1998): 124-133.

WALKING THE PATH OF DIALOGUE IN ASIA
FABC Wisdom on Interreligious Dialogue

Concrete facts and statistics are most helpful in grasping the enormous challenges facing the Church in Asia. Current Asian statistics may surprise and startle us; they should shake our complacency. In a word, these realities concretize the task at hand: *bringing the light and power of the Gospel into the multi-religious and pluri-cultural reality of contemporary Asia*.

Asia, the world's largest and most populated continent, constitutes one third of the world's land area (17,124,000 square miles) and is home to almost 60% of humanity. It is a continent of the young (about 40% are below 15 years of age); there are more than 30 mega-cities in Asia with populations ranging from 5 to 20 million. The nine most populous nations (in descending order) are: China, India, Indonesia, Japan, Bangladesh, Pakistan, Vietnam, Philippines, and Thailand. China's population exceeds one billion; India's populace crossed the one billion mark in the year 2000. With this massive bulk goes a wide variety of diversity and contrasts—physical, ethnic, social, economic, cultural, political, and religious.

Asia is a continent rich in non-Christian cultures. It is the homeland of three eminent world religions: Hinduism, Buddhism, and Islam; 85% of all the world's non-Christians are in Asia and they adhere to several of the great religions. Hinduism, born about 5,000 years ago, has about 650 million followers, most of them in India and neighboring countries. Buddhism is a religion and philosophy developed from Hinduism by Siddhartha Gautama, (the "Enlightened One"); it has 300 million followers, mostly in Asia.

Islam, established by the prophet Muhammad in the seventh century, is a monotheistic religion; it incorporates elements of Judaic and Christian belief. Islam numbers over 700 million followers in Asia alone; the Catholics of Asia are slightly over 120 million. Significantly, well over 50% of Asian Catholics are found in one country alone—the Philippines; thus, Catholics in most Asian nations are a small—even tiny—minority (frequently less that 1%). The four largest Islamic nations in the world, each with over 100 million Muslims, are found in Asia: Indonesia (216m), Pakistan (161m), India 147m), and Bangladesh (122m) [2007 statistics]. Other significant religious and philosophical-ethical systems in Asia are Confucianism, Taoism, Shintoism, as well as many indigenous, traditional belief systems.

Catholic Church in Asia. Catholics worldwide constitute 17.2% of all people; all Christians are 33.1% of humanity. Catholics in Asia (approximately 120+ million) represent only 2.9% of the over 3.5 billion Asians. The Church in Asia continues to grow. In 1988 there were 84.3 million Catholics; now they have reached 120+ million (an increase of about 25%). The number of priests rose from 27,700 to 32,291 during the same period. Asian countries with the most seminarians (given in descending order) are: India, Philippines, South Korea, and Vietnam. The vast majority (86%) of religious sisters are also Asian; countries with the largest number of indigenous sisters (in descending rank) are: India, Philippines, South Korea, Japan, Indonesia, and Vietnam. The Church in Asia is known publicly for its commitment to education, health care, and social services.

Regarding the individual nations in the region covered by the Federation of Asian Bishops' Conferences (FABC), abundant statistics are available; only two items are presented here. For each FABC country listed the *estimated population* in millions at the *beginning* of the third millennium is listed; this is followed by the *percentage of Catholics* in that nation (a statistic that shows little change, even as the total population increases): **Bangladesh** (145.8m / 0.27%); **Bhutan** (1.8m / 0.02%); **Burma/ Myanmar** (48.8m / 1.3%); **Cambodia** (10.3m / 0.02%); **China**

(1,239.5m / 0.5%); **Hong Kong** (6.9m / 4.7%); India (1,000m / 1.72%); **Indonesia** (202m / 2.58%); **Japan** (127.7m / 0.36%); **Korea-North** (22.6m / ?); **Korea-South** (47.2m / 6.7%); **Laos** (6.2m / 0.9%); **Macau** (0.5m / 5%); **Malaysia** (22m / 3%); **Mongolia** (2.5m / ?); **Nepal** (23m / 0.05%); **Pakistan** (142.6m / 0.6%); **Philippines** (76.2m / 81%); **Singapore** (3.1m / 6.5%); **Sri Lanka** (20.8m / 8%); **Taiwan** (22.1m / 1.4%); **Thailand** (61.6m / 0.4%); **Vietnam** (78.2m / 6.1%).

These few secular and religious statistics already indicate that "being a missionary Church in Asia" demands creative, innovative, *dialogical* and *inculturated* approaches to Gospel proclamation. Local Churches must consider diverse cultural, religious, political, social and economic realities as they envision a pastoral program of integral and dialogical evangelization. The task before the Churches is great; they must respond with enthusiasm and insight!

An Asian Perspective. The Church in Asia, like anywhere in the world, necessarily seeks to accomplish her mission within a definite context. The great diversity and uniqueness across Asia on many levels has already been noted; several studies would be needed to explore the many facets of the evangelization process in Asia. This current study focuses on the broad area on religions and dialogue in Asia, and it is presented from the perspective of Asia's bishops (FABC).

This presentation will include several sections. *First*, a brief introduction to the Federation of Asian Bishops' Conferences (FABC) will be presented; *second*, drawing on the insights of the FABC on religions and dialogue, the missiological foundations for dialogue will be unfolded in five sections; *third*, employing the FABC wisdom, principles of praxis for dialogue will be presented in five points; *fourth*, a personal "interfaith" experience will be narrated; *finally*, a modest bibliography will be presented, drawing upon FABC material as well as important "Asian" theologians and missiologists; the sources include indigenous authors and expatriate missionaries—all of whom have a "heart" for Asia.

This approach [separating the original FABC documents (sections two and three) from the works of theologians (section five)] has been chosen so that the original insights of the FABC will be retained in their originality. This author finds that the FABC texts themselves are very insightful and eloquent; they are poetic; they are visionary, inspiring, and soul-stirring. Thus, this author prefers to extensively quote the original material, rather than mix commentaries by theologians and missiologists with the FABC texts themselves. And, at the same time, hoping not to lose the profound insights of the theologians, their works are cited in the bibliographical section, which simply follows an alphabetical and chronological arrangement.

Readers will find the quoted FABC material referenced in two ways. The original FABC source will be provided in the text, using abbreviations and numerical references; an example is the following: [*Source*: FABC I (Taipei): 8]. This reference enables a reader to find the original quote, regardless of the printed version or possible translation. Following this first source, a reference will be given to the five-volume collection of FABC documents, *For All the Peoples of Asia* [*FAPA*]; this series, published by the Claretians in Manila and Orbis Books of Maryknoll, NY, is the standard reference tool for FABC sources. In addition, the two-volume resource, which presents all the FABC doctoral studies written from 1985-2008, can serve as a useful source-book; also published by the Claretians in Manila, it bears the title *Theology from the Heart of Asia*.

BRIEF FABC INTRODUCTION

The Federation of Asian Bishops' Conferences (FABC) is a transnational episcopal structure that brings together bishops from twenty-eight Asian countries; it grew out of the historic gathering of 180 Asian Catholic Bishops with Pope Paul VI during his 1970 Asian visit.

FABC has a modest central structure; there are also nine FABC offices, which carry out many concrete initiatives and projects. These offices, scattered among various Asian nations, are focused on evangelization, social communication, laity, human development, education and student chaplaincy, ecumenical and interreligious affairs, theological concerns, clergy, and consecrated life. Through their diverse activities such as seminars and publications, each of these offices promotes the growth of the Asian local Churches.

The supreme body of the FABC is the Plenary Assembly, which convenes every four years. To date, ten plenary assemblies have been held (see previous chapter on inculturation for details). The FABC central secretariat publishes the *FABC Papers*; they are available in print form or in pdf format on the FABC website; see numbers 100 and 125 for comprehensive indexes.

Succinctly, one may validly assert that the FABC has been the most influential body in the Asian Church since the Second Vatican Council. It has strengthened the bonds of communication among the bishops in the region and has contributed to the development of a shared vision about the Church and her evangelizing mission in Asia (copious FABC quotes in this presentation will reveal the depths of this FABC vision). For the Church in Asia to truly discover its own identity it must continually engage in a three-fold dialogue with the peoples (especially the poor), the cultures, and the religions of Asia [the focused subject of this presentation]. This programmatic vision has guided the FABC for over four decades. One can validly assert that the FABC is truly "Asia's Continuing Vatican II."

MISSIOLOGICAL FOUNDATIONS OF
INTERFAITH DIALOGUE

I. Church's Commitment to Missionary Evangelization in Asia. The Catholic Church in Asia is committed to bring the Good News to Asian peoples. However, local Christians are not always fully involved in this mission. The FABC documents assert that: "... the preaching of Jesus Christ and His Gospel to our peoples in Asia becomes a task which today assumes an urgency, a necessity and magnitude unmatched in the history of our Faith in this part of the world. It is because of this that we can repeat the Apostle's word, and repeat it joyfully, 'Woe to me if I do not preach the Gospel,' (I Cor. 9:16) for it is 'the love of Christ which presses us' (II Cor. 5:14) to share with our peoples what is most precious in our hearts and in our lives, Jesus Christ and his Gospel, the unsurpassable riches of Christ (cf. Eph. 3:8)." [*Source*: FABC I (Taipei): 8] (*FAPA I*, 13-14).

Asian Christians believe that: "... it is as *servants of the Lord* and of *humanity* that we Christians share the same journey with all the Asian peoples. The Church was not sent to observe but to serve—to serve the Asian peoples in their quest for God and for a better human life; to serve Asia under the leading of the Spirit of Christ and in the manner of Christ himself who did not come to be served but to serve and to lay down his life as a ransom for all (Mk. 10:45)—and to discern, in dialogue with Asian peoples and Asian realities, what deeds the Lord wills to be done so that all humankind may be gathered together in harmony as his family. As servant of Yahweh and of humanity, the Church will seek above all faithfulness to God and to the Asian peoples, and will also invite to full participation in the Christian community those who are lead to it by the Spirit of God." [*Source*: FABC V (Bandung): 6:3] (*FAPA I*, 283).

The Church in Asia admits its limitations: "... how insufficient for the most part has been our missionary consciousness and responsibility. We have so frequently forgotten that the summons and challenge to make known the person and message of Jesus Christ to those who do not know him is a mandate addressed to even the youngest Christian community." [*Source*: FABC III (Bangkok): 9:9] (*FAPA I*, 58). "Unfortunately for many Catholics, faith is only something to be received and celebrated. They do not feel it is something to be shared. The missionary nature of the gift of faith must be inculcated in all Christians." [*Source*: FABC V (Bandung): 3.2.3] (*FAPA I*, 280).

II. FABC's Vision of Integral Evangelization. This task

of evangelization is holistic and comprehensive in its scope; Pope Paul VI noted: "For the Church, evangelizing means bringing the Good News into all the strata of humanity, and through its influence transforming humanity from within and making it new." [*Source*: Paul VI, *Evangelii Nuntiandi* 18]. FABC describes missionary evangelization: "Mission, being a continuation in the Spirit of the mission of Christ, involves a being with people, as was Jesus: 'The Word became flesh and dwelt among us' (Jn. 1:14)." [*Source*: FABC V (Bandung): 3.1.2] (*FAPA I*, 280). "Evangelization is the carrying out of the Church's duty of proclaiming by word and witness the Gospel of the Lord." [*Source*: FABC I (Taipei): 25] (*FAPA I*, 16).

The **content** of evangelization is noted: "… mission includes: being with the people, responding to their needs, with sensitiveness to the presence of God in cultures and other religious traditions, and witnessing to the values of God's Kingdom through presence, solidarity, sharing and word. Mission will mean a dialogue with Asia's poor, with its local cultures, and with other religious traditions (FABC I)." [*Source*: FABC V (Bandung): 3.1.2] (*FAPA I*, 280).

"Local Churches, servant and inculturated, are the subject of the evangelizing mission…. The principal elements [are] as follows: 1) simple presence and living witness; 2) concrete commitment to the service of humankind; … 3) liturgical life … prayer and contemplation; 4) dialogue in which Christians meet the followers of other religious traditions; … 5) proclamation and catechesis…. The totality of Christian mission embraces all these elements." [*Source*: CTC (Hua Hin, 1991): 36] (*FAPA I*, 343).

"Integral Evangelization requires that we become witnesses in our lives to the values and norms of the Gospel based on our baptismal consecration." [*Source*: SFMWA (Hong Kong): 28] (*FAPA II*, 54).

The FABC has also spoken about the **motivation** for missionary evangelization: "Renewal of a sense of mission will also require a renewal of our motivations for mission. There has been perceived in some way a weakening of these motivations so necessary to persevere in this demanding task. Why indeed, should we evangelize? ... a) We evangelize, first of all, from a deep sense of *gratitude to God*.... b) But, mission is also a *mandate*.... c) We evangelize also because we *believe* in the Lord Jesus.... d) We evangelize also because we have been *incorporated by baptism into the Church*, which is missionary by its very nature.... e) And finally, we evangelize because the Gospel is *leaven* for liberation and for the transformation of society." [*Source*: FABC V (Bandung): 3.2] (*FAPA I*, 280-281).

III. Announcing the Person and Promises of Christ. The Churches of Asia see a clear Christological component to evangelization; they assert: "While we are aware and sensitive to the fact that evangelization is a complex reality and has many essential aspects—such a witnessing to the Gospel, working for the values of the Kingdom, struggling along with those who strive for justice and peace, dialogue, sharing, inculturation, mutual enrichment with other Christians and the followers of all religions—we affirm that there can never be true evangelization without the proclamation of Jesus Christ. The proclamation of Jesus Christ is the center and the primary element of evangelization without which all other elements will lose their cohesion and validity." [*Source*: BIMA I (Suwon): 5-6] (*FAPA I*, 292).

"It is true that in many places Christ cannot yet be proclaimed openly by words. But He can, and should be, proclaimed through other ways, namely: through the witness of the life of the Christian community and family, and their striving to know and live more fully the faith they profess; through their desire to live in peace and harmony with those who do not share our faith.... Our proclamation of Jesus must also be urgently directed towards the workers, the poor and needy, and the oppressed...." [*Source*: BIMA III (Changhua): 10-11] (*FAPA I*, 105).

FABC continues: "... challenged by the stark reality of

millions on our continent who have not yet been evangelized, we welcome ... this opportunity to face with a sense of urgency the task of making Christ known, loved and followed by the vast multitude of our brothers and sisters." [*Source*: BIMA I (Baguio): 2] (*FAPA I*, 93). "More than two billions of Asians have perhaps never encountered the Person of Jesus in a knowing and conscious way; more than two billions of Asians have never really heard His message. While this fact fills us with sorrow, it also spurs us on to longing and hope, because we know He will accompany the ways of all those whose footsteps are lovely because they bring the good news of His mercy and love." [*Source*: BIMA III (Changhua): 4] (*FAPA I*, 104).

"We affirm ... that 'the proclamation of Jesus Christ is the center and primary element of evangelization.' ... But the proclamation of Jesus Christ in Asia means, first of all, the witness of Christians and of Christian communities to the values of the Kingdom of God, *a proclamation through Christ-like deeds*. For Christians in Asia, to proclaim Christ means above all to live like him, in the midst of our neighbors of other faiths and persuasions, and to do his deeds by the power of his grace. Proclamation through dialogue and deeds—this is the first call to the Churches in Asia." [*Source*: FABC V (Bandung): 4.1] (*FAPA I*, 281-282). "The local Churches of Asia will proclaim Jesus Christ to their fellow humans in a dialogical manner." [*Source*: CTC (Hua Hin): 51] (*FAPA I*, 346).

IV. Interfaith Dialogue as a Key Dimension of Mission. Asia's bishops have a deep appreciation of the role of dialogue in the evangelization process; they hold: "Interreligious dialogue is another integral part of evangelization which in the situation of our Churches needs to become a primary concern. We live in the midst of millions of people belonging to the great religious traditions.... In this context we believe that interreligious dialogue is a true expression of the Church's evangelizing action in which the mystery of Jesus Christ is operative, calling us all to conversion.... We would wish to see interreligious dialogue become a reality at the grassroots level of our Church, through greater openness and reaching out of all their members towards their brothers and sisters of other religious traditions." [*Source*: BIMA II (Trivandrum): 14] (*FAPA I*, 100-101).

"The Church, the sacrament of God's message in the world, continues Christ's work of dialogue…. The Church is particularly concerned with man's religious experience, the motivating and leavening agent in his culture. This means that the Church must constantly be involved in dialogue with men of other religions (cf. *Nostra Aetate* 2). The Christian finds himself continually evangelizing and being evangelized by his partners in dialogue (cf. *Evangelii Nuntiandi* 13)." [*Source*: BIRA II (Kuala Lumpur): 11] (*FAPA I*, 115). Therefore, "It suffices for the present to indicate here the continued building up of the local church as the focus of the task of evangelization today, with dialogue as its essential mode, … through interreligious dialogue undertaken in all seriousness." [*Source*: IMC (Manila): 19] (*FAPA I*, 131).

Indeed, since the Church in Asia is a "small flock," the FABC insightfully asserts: "Mission may find its greatest urgency in Asia: it also finds in our continent a distinctive mode: [dialogue]." [*Source*: FABC V (Bandung): 4.1] (*FAPA I*, 281). "From our experience of dialogue emerged the conviction that *dialogue was the key we sought*—not dialogue in the superficial sense in which it is often understood, but as a witnessing to Christ in word and deed, by reaching out to people in the concrete reality of their daily lives…." [*Source*: BIMA I (Baguio): 5] (*FAPA I*, 94). "In the context of dialogue we tried to penetrate the meaning of the uniqueness of Christ—in our own inner experience, in our contact with others; … we realized that there is still much to be discovered, and much that is already discovered but not sufficiently integrated in our lives and in our missionary effort…. We feel that the Christian experience in contact with the age-old religious experience of Asia has much to contribute to the growth and the transformation in outlook and appearance of the Universal Church." [*Source*: BIMA I (Baguio): 12] (*FAPA I*, 94-95).

FABC adds an important point of clarification: "Dialogue does not call for giving up one's commitment, bracketing it or entering into easy compromise. On the contrary, for a deeper and fruitful dialogue, it is even necessary that each partner be firmly committed to his or her faith." [*Source*: BIRA IV/7 (Tagaytay): 10] (*FAPA I*, 309-310). "Dialogue within the Church is important and it is this attitude that will lead us to respect others and to understand evangelization as a process of listening to what they are expressing in and through their lives of the goodness of the Almighty God. It is clear that Dialogue is not for Conversion." [*Source*: FIESA IV (Kuala Lumpur): 12] (*FAPA IV*, 86).

V. God's Saving Design is at Work in the Asian Reality. FABC documents are premised on a broad vision of God's loving plan of salvation; thus, "Christians believe that God's saving will is at work, in many different ways, in all religions. It has been recognized since the time of the apostolic Church, and stated clearly again by the Second Vatican Council (cf. *Gaudium et Spes* 22; *Lumen Gentium* 16), that the Spirit of Christ is active outside the bounds of the visible Church (cf. *Redemptor Hominis* 6). God's saving grace is not limited to members of the Church, but is offered to every person.... His ways are mysterious and unfathomable, and no one can dictate the direction of His grace." [*Source*: BIRA II (Kuala Lumpur): 12] (*FAPA I*, 115).

"God, the Father of all, has called all men to share in his life and love through his son Jesus Christ. The risen Christ and his Spirit are active in the world making this love a present and growing reality, making all things new. This same love urges us on to dialogue with people of other religions, because we have, especially since the Second Vatican Council, an increasing awareness of the positive role of other religions in God's plan of salvation." [*Source*: BIRA III (Madras): 2] (*FAPA I*, 119).

FABC continues: "In Asia especially this involves a dialogue with the great religious traditions of our peoples. In this dialogue we accept them as significant and positive elements in the economy of God's design of salvation." [*Source*: FABC I (Taipei): 14] (*FAPA I*, 14). And again: "... a clearer perception of the Church's mission in the context of the Asian reality helps us discover even deeper motivations. Members of other religious traditions already in some way share with us in the mystery of salvation." [*Source*: CTC (Hua Hin): 50] (*FAPA I*, 346). Furthermore: "We are glad that Vatican II affirmed the presence of salvific values in other religions. We are grateful for the timely insights.... The Gospel fulfills all hopes, a Gospel which Asia and the whole world direly need." [*Source*: BIMA I (Suwon): 7] (*FAPA I*, 292).

On this theme Saint John Paul II has written: "The Spirit's presence and activity affect not only individuals, but also society and history, peoples, cultures and religions.... The Church's relationship with other religions is dictated by a twofold respect: 'Respect for man in his quest for answers to the deepest questions of his life, and respect for the action of the Spirit in man." [*Source: Redemptoris Missio*: 28-29]. Within the awareness of the Holy Spirit's action and their commitment to dialogue, Asia's bishops boldly state: "... we shall not be timid when God opens the door for us to *proclaim* explicitly the Lord Jesus Christ as the Savior and the answer to the fundamental questions of human existence." [*Source*: FABC V (Bandung): 4.3] (*FAPA I*, 282).

DIALOGUE PRAXIS IN THE ASIAN CONTEXT

I.   Basic Attitudes Essential to Dialogue Practice. The commitment of Asia's bishops to interfaith dialogue is clear and consistent; the FABC enunciates foundational attitudes essential to this dialogue. "In Asia, the emphasis in interreligious dialogue falls not so much on academic or theological discussions, as on the sharing of life at all levels. Christians carry out the mission entrusted to them by Jesus Christ when they participate fully in the social and cultural life of the societies in which they live, enriching others by the values they have learned from the Gospel, and finding themselves enriched by the spiritual treasures of their neighbors of other faiths. Thus, the 'dialogue of life' is central to Christian life in Asia…. Christians in Asia are called to live their faith deeply, in openness and respect for the religious commitment of others." [*Source*: FIRA IV (Pattaya): 4] (*FAPA III*, 140).

Dialogue demands transformed attitudes: "… to be able to engage in genuine interreligious dialogue, we need to deepen our self-knowledge and continuously discover our personal identity…. we need to be continually healed of negativities like suspicion and fear…. in order to go deeper into ourselves in this inward journey to the God of the Ongoing Dialogue, we need to integrate Asian forms of prayer…. We acknowledge here the tremendous opportunities we have of learning from the other religious traditions of Asia, especially from the mystical traditions." [*Source*: FIRA I (Ipoh): 3.2-3.3] (*FAPA III*, 122).

"Any dialogical enterprise requires certain basic attitudes, as exemplified in Christ: — a spirit of humility, openness, receptivity, and … for what God wishes to tell us through them [Asia's religions]; —a witnessing to the saving grace of Christ, not so much by the proclaimed word but through love in the Christian community, so that its universal validity is seen and felt as such; —a placing of priority on fellowship…, so that we are led spontaneously and naturally to deeper religious dialogue." [*Source*: BIRA I (Bangkok): 18] (*FAPA I*, 111).

FABC promotes a balanced appreciation of dialogue: "… for a deeper and fruitful dialogue, it is even necessary that each partner be firmly committed to his or her faith…. While firmly adhering to our commitment to Christ, it is indispensable for dialogue that we enter into the religious universe of our dialogue partner and see his or her sincere and unflinching faith-commitment. More than that, we should appreciate the commitment of the other…. That is why listening attentively with our heart to the personal commitment of faith and witness of the other partner can not only facilitate dialogue, but also enrich us and make us grow in our faith, and help us to reinterpret it." [*Source*: BIRA IV/7 (Tagaytay): 10-11] (*FAPA I*, 309-310).

"Dialogue is a crucial challenge to the Churches in Asia in their growing commitment to the building of the kingdom. This challenge is fraught with risks.... However, with the confidence that the Spirit is with us and helps us in our weakness (Rom. 8:26), we commit ourselves to this task of dialogue...." [*Source*: BIRA III (Madras): Conclusion] (*FAPA I*, 123).

II. Specific Attitudes toward Asia's Venerable Religions. The FABC in its first plenary gathering enunciated a profound— even poetic—appraisal of Asia's religions: "In this dialogue we accept them as significant and positive elements in the economy of God's design of salvation. In them we recognize and respect profound spiritual and ethical meanings and values. Over many centuries they have been the treasury of the religious experience of our ancestors, from which our contemporaries do not cease to draw light and strength. They have been (and continue to be) the authentic expression of the noblest longings of their hearts, and the home of their contemplation and prayer. They have helped to give shape to the histories and cultures of our nations." [*Source*: FABC I (Taipei): 14] (*FAPA I*, 14). "How then can we not give them reverence and honor? And how can we not acknowledge that God has drawn our peoples to Himself through them?" [*Source*: FABC I (Taipei): 15] (*FAPA I*, 14).

"Only in dialogue with these religions can we discover in them the seeds of the Word of God (*Ad Gentes* 9). This dialogue will allow us to touch the expression and the reality of our peoples' deepest selves, and enable us to find authentic ways of living and expressing our own Christian faith. It will reveal to us also many riches of our own faith which we perhaps would not have perceived. Thus it can become a sharing in friendship of our quest for God and for brotherhood among His sons." [*Source*: FABC I (Taipei): 16] (*FAPA I*, 14-15). "Finally, this dialogue will teach us what our faith in Christ leads us to receive from these religious traditions, and what must be purified in them, healed and made whole, in the light of God's Word." [*Source*: FABC I (Taipei): 17] (*FAPA I*, 15).

Asia's bishops continue: "On our part we can offer what we believe the Church alone has the duty and joy to offer to them and to all men: oneness with the Father in Jesus His Son; the ways to grace Christ gives us in His Gospel and His sacraments, and in the fellowship of the community which seeks to live in Him; an understanding too of the value of the human person and of the social dimensions of human salvation—a salvation which assumes and gives meaning to human freedom, earthly realities, and the course of this world's history." [*Source*: FABC I (Taipei): 18] (*FAPA I*, 15).

III. Necessity of a "Spirituality of Dialogue." For over four decades the FABC has asserted that spirituality is linked to authentic dialogue: "In Asia, home to great religions, where individuals and entire peoples are thirsting for the divine, the Church is called to be a praying Church, deeply spiritual, even as she engages in immediate human and social concerns. All Christians need a true missionary spirituality of prayer and contemplation." [*Source*: FABC VII (Samphran): C-2] (*FAPA III*, 13).

"At the center of this new way of being Church [in Asia] is the action of the Spirit of Jesus, guiding and directing individual believers as well as the whole community to live a life that is Spirit-filled—that is, to live an authentic spirituality. It is nothing more and nothing less than a following of Jesus-in-mission, an authentic discipleship in the context of Asia." [*Source*: FABC V (Bandung): 9:1] (*FAPA I*, 288).

"To risk being wounded in the act of loving, to seek to understand in a climate of misunderstanding—these are no light burdens to bear. Dialogue demands a deep spirituality which enables man, as did Jesus Christ, to hang on to his faith in God's love, even when everything seems to fall apart. Dialogue, finally, demands a total Christ-like self-emptying so that, led by the Spirit, we may be more effective instruments in building up God's Kingdom." [*Source*: BIRA IV/7 (Tagaytay): 16] (*FAPA I*, 311).

"In Asia, the dialogue of prayer and spirituality is highly valued. Prayer together, in ways congruent with the faith of those who take part, is an occasion for Christians and followers of other faiths to appreciate better the spiritual riches which each group possesses, as well as to grow in respect for one another as fellow pilgrims on the path through life. Human solidarity is deepened when people approach the divine as one human family." [*Source*: FIRA IV (Pattaya): 8] (*FAPA III*, 141). At the First Asian Mission Congress in 2006, the participants committed themselves to "living and promoting a spirituality of the dialogue of life with the peoples of Asia." [*Source*: AMC I (Chiang Mai): Orientations, Part One] (*FAPA IV*, 280).

The Asian bishops have a "friend of dialogue" in the person of John Paul II (see *Redemptoris Missio* [RM] 55-57); elsewhere in the same document the pope has written: "... the interreligious meeting held in Assisi was meant to confirm my conviction that 'every authentic prayer is prompted by the Holy Spirit, who is mysteriously present in every human heart'." [*Source*: RM 29].

Asia's bishops face the challenge of dialogue with realism: "Interreligious dialogue is never easy, it calls for its own spirituality. It is our resolve, therefore, to live and witness to this spirituality of dialogue...." [*Source*: FIRA I (Ipoh): 4.2] (*FAPA III*, 124). "... credible evangelization demands from us Christians in Asia a life of authentic contemplation and genuine compassion.... Only an ego-emptying, and consequently powerless, Christian community has the credibility to proclaim the folly of the message of the cross. Such a process of evangelization fosters a culture of dialogue in Asia." [*Source*: FEISA I (Pattaya): 7.4.1-2] (*FAPA II*, 61). Finally, "The call of the laity to holiness and consequently, to the apostolate of the Church..., is a demand of their Christian identity in virtue of the Christian's full incorporation into Christ and in the Holy Eucharist." [*Source*: BILA III (Singapore): 6] (*FAPA I*, 244).

IV. Dialogue Serves a New Humanity and the Kingdom.
FABC asserts that dialogue is always oriented outward in service
of people and God's kingdom. "Dialogue is a crucial challenge
to the Churches in Asia in their growing commitment to the
building of the kingdom. This challenge is fraught with risks
arising out of confusing socio-political tensions, besides other
causes. However, with the confidence that the Spirit is with us
and helps us in our weakness (Rom. 8:26), we commit ourselves
to this task of dialogue in order to unite the whole universe in
Christ so that God may be all in all (I Cor. 15:28)." [*Source*:
BIRA III (Madras): Conclusion] (*FAPA I*, 123).

"We build the Church in order to build the Kingdom in our
Asian societies and cultures.... Our mission therefore must be a
dialogue with those of other religious ways that will require us
both to proclaim and be proclaimed to, to speak and to listen,
to teach and to learn. Through such a dialogical mission, God's
Reign will grow in Asia and the Church will become more truly
an Asian Church, inculturated in Asian realities." [*Source*: FIRA
II (Pattaya): 3.5] (*FAPA III*, 128).

"The Kingdom of God is therefore universally present and
at work. Wherever men and women open themselves to the
transcendent divine mystery which impinges upon them and
go out of themselves in love and service to fellow humans,
there the reign of God is at work.... This goes to show that
the Reign of God is a universal reality, extending far beyond
the boundaries of the Church. It is the reality of salvation in
Jesus Christ, in which Christians and others share together.
It is the fundamental 'mystery of unity' which unites us more
deeply than differences in religious allegiance are able to keep
us apart." [*Source*: CTC (Hua Hin): 29-30] (*FAPA I*, 341-342).

With clear resolve, Asia's bishops state: "Therefore, we
commit ourselves: ...To take every opportunity to make Jesus
Christ and his message known in a way that is acceptable to
Asians, presenting him to them with an 'Asian face,' using Asian
cultural concepts, terms and symbols; ... To present the Gospel
message as humble servants of the Kingdom of God, always

sensitive to the religious and cultural traditions of the people where the Spirit leads us to make Jesus known." [*Source*: AMSAL I (Tagaytay): 2] (*FAPA III*, 206).

"This common spiritual pilgrimage demands that we take inspiration from the praxis of Jesus, especially his table fellowship with publicans and sinners, wherein we discover the primal form of the Church of Christ. Before Christianity got established as a structured religion, it was a spiritual movement: Jesus' journey with the poor towards the Kingdom of God. In close dialogue with the poor and the religious cultures of Asia, the Church would be able to rediscover its pristine dynamism which demands a radical emptying (*kenosis*) in its thought patterns, ritual forms and community structures. This age of journeying with sisters and brothers of Asian religions is a privileged moment (*kairos*) for the Church to return to its original call." [*Source*: FEISA I (Pattaya): 7.5.1] (*FAPA II*, 61).

V. Local Church: Identity, Ministries, and Service. To promote and concretize this dialogical vision, the FABC links its implementation with Asia's local Churches and their ministries. "Each local Church is determined by her human context and lives in a dialectical relationship with the human society into which she is inserted as the Gospel leaven. Since each local Church should embody into the context the task entrusted to her by the servant Lord, she has to discover time and again what ministries and what ministerial structures she requires in order to fulfill her mission to offer to a human society the salvation brought about by Jesus Christ...." [*Source*: ACMC (Hong Kong): 25] (*FAPA I*, 72).

"The renewal of our sense of mission will mean ... that the acting subject of mission is the *local church* living and acting in communion with the universal Church. It is the local churches and communities which can discern and work out ... the way the Gospel is best proclaimed, the Church set up, the values of God's Kingdom realized in their own place and time. In fact, it is by responding to and serving the needs of the peoples of

Asia that the different Christian communities become truly local churches." [*Source*: FABC V (Bandung): 3.3.1] (*FAPA I*, 281).

The FABC forcefully asserts: "Asian Churches then must become truly Asian in all things. The principle of indigenization and inculturation is at the very root of their coming into their own. The ministry of Asian Churches, if it is to be authentic, must be relevant to Asian societies. This calls on the part of the Churches for originality, creativity and inventiveness, for boldness and courage." [*Source*: ACMC (Hong Kong): 26] (*FAPA I*, 72-73).

"Now—as Vatican II already affirmed with all clarity and force—every local church is and cannot be but missionary. Every local church is 'sent' by Christ and the Father to bring the Gospel to its surrounding milieu, and to bear it also into all the world. For every local church this is a *primary task*.... Every local church is responsible for its mission...." [*Source*: IMC (Manila): 14] (*FAPA I*, 130).

With great conviction, Asia's bishops state: "... the decisive new phenomenon for Christianity in Asia will be the emergence of genuine Christian communities in Asia—Asian in their way of thinking, praying, living, communicating their own Christ-experience to others. The consequences will be tremendous ... [in] all aspects of their life.... If the Asian Churches do not discover their own identity, they will have no future." [*Source*: ACMC (Hong Kong): 14] (*FAPA I*, 70).

"Each local church has its own vocation in the one history of salvation, in the one Church of Christ. In each local church each people's history, each people's culture, meanings and values, each people's traditions are taken up, not diminished or destroyed, but celebrated and renewed, purified if need be, and fulfilled ... in the life of the Spirit." [*Source*: IMC (Manila): 15] (*FAPA I*, 130).

A BANGLADESHI BEGGAR WOMAN

In light of the foregoing presentation of the FABC's profound understanding of the Church's mission of fostering relationships and dialogue with Asia's religions, this "Asian panorama of dialogue" presents an integrating quote and the narration of a true experience. Pope John Paul II, speaking in Manila to the peoples of Asia during his 1981 Philippine visit (5), asserted that the goal of interfaith dialogue should be altruistic (not focused only on personal enrichment); he stated: "Christians will, moreover, join hands with all men and women of good will ... [and] work together in order to bring about a more just and peaceful society in which the poor will be the first to be served." Yes, the Asian way of mission is *dialogical service of the needy*; this approach can clearly reveal the face of Jesus in Asia today. This was poignantly brought home to this author in a transforming experience that I consider a gift of the Lord to me.

During the Lenten season some few years ago, while I was a visiting professor in Dhaka, Bangladesh, I had a "graced moment," a "defining experience" in my missionary awareness and perspective. It has remained seared in my consciousness and has forced me to ask many foundational questions about faith, mission and my own commitment. It involves a Bangladeshi beggar woman.

I saw her on the road, in front of the large walled compound of a wealthy family dwelling. I could not clearly see her face, as she was several hundred feet ahead of me. Her tattered clothes covered a malnourished body; she was alone, although other beggars were walking ahead of her on the road. I was proceeding along the same path, leisurely taking a late afternoon walk.

Suddenly a luxury car approached with its horn blowing. The driver probably wanted the beggars to disperse and also wanted the gate of the compound opened by the servants.

The woman appeared startled as the car turned sharply in front of her and the gate swung open. Within seconds two large dogs emerged from the compound and jumped at the woman, knocking her to the ground. She screamed and cried both from fear and the pain caused by the dogs nipping at her. I stood frozen, horrified at the sight.

A well-dressed madam promptly emerged from the chauffeur-driven car. She ordered the driver to bring the car into the compound; the dogs were called to return inside; the servants were commanded to close and lock the gate. And, the beggar woman? She was left alone on the ground—outside the gate. I stood helpless, gazing at this appalling scene.

Only the other frightened beggars came to the aid of the woman. Only they showed mercy and compassion. I stood at a distance and wept at this scene of crucifixion. I admitted to being a guilty bystander. My fears and inadequacies left me paralyzed. I had not one *taka* coin in my pocket to give; I could not offer one word of consolation in the Bengali language which I did not speak; I did not approach the woman for fear of misinterpretation that a foreign man would touch a Bengali woman in public in this strictly Islamic culture. I simply wept in solidarity. I wept long and hard. And, in succeeding years, I have frequently returned to that scene and prayed to God: "Do not let me forget that experience. Allow it to shape my life and mission vision. Permit it to remain a 'defining moment' in understanding my mission vocation."

My Christian faith, along with the insights of FABC, provide me with a vision to interpret this experience. I believe in a God is who radically compassionate to everyone—Muslim, Hindu, Buddhist, Christian. Thus, relying on God's grace, I look forward to meeting once again that Muslim Bangladeshi beggar-woman—she who so deeply shared in the paschal mystery—in the resurrected life with Christ the Lord in heaven. I am confident she will be there!

ABBREVIATIONS

ACMC - Asian Colloquium on Ministries in the Church
AMC - Asian Mission Congress (Chiang Mai – 2006)
AMSAL - Asian-born Missionary Societies of Apostolic Life
BILA - Bishops' Institute for Lay Apostolate
BIMA - Bishops' Institute for Missionary Apostolate
BIRA - Bishops' Institute for Interreligious Affairs
CTC - Conclusions of Theological Consultation (Hua Hin, 1994)
EN - *Evangelii Nuntiandi*
FABC - Federation of Asian Bishops' Conferences
FEISA - Faith Encounters in Asia
FIRA - Formation Institute for Interreligious Affairs
IMC - International Mission Congress (Manila – 1979)
RM - *Redemptoris Missio*
SFMWA - Statement on Filipino Migrant Workers in Asia

NOTE: All these abbreviations are used in the body of the text and they refer to FABC documents found in the five volumes of *For All the Peoples of Asia*, produced by Claretian Publications in Quezon City (Metro Manila), Philippines and Orbis Books of Maryknoll, NY.

RELIGIONS AND DIALOGUE IN ASIA
A Focused Bibliography

Almario, C. (Ed.). *Evangelization in Asia: Proceedings of the Asian Congress on Evangelization.* Quezon City, Philippines: Claretian Publications, 1993.

Amaladoss, A. **(A)** "The Spirituality of Dialogue," *Studies in Interreligious Dialogue* 3 (1993): 58-70; **(B)** "Interreligious Dialogue: A View from Asia," *International Bulletin of Missionary Research* 19 (1995): 2-5; **(C)** "Dialogue between Religions in Asia Today," *East Asian Pastoral Review* 42 (2005): 45-60; **(D)** "Other

Religions and the Salvific Mystery of Christ," *Vidyajyoti* 70 (2006): 8-23.

Arinze, F. **(A)** *The Church in Dialogue: Walking with Other Believers*. San Francisco: Ignatius Press, 1990; **(B)** *Meeting Other Believers*. Shillong, India: Vendrame Institute Publications, 1998; **(C)** "The Rich Religious Dimension of Tribal Religions," *Pro Dialogo* 99 (1998): 289-294; **(D)** "Interreligious Dialogue in the Third Millennium," *Studia Missionalia* 48 (1999): 203-213.

Bevans, S. "Inculturation of Theology in Asia: The FABC 1970-1995," *Studia Missionalia* 45 (1996): 1-23.

Borelli, J. "John Paul II and Interreligious Dialogue," In *The Wojtyla Years* [*New Catholic Encyclopedia XX*]. **J. Komonchak** *et al.* (Eds.)., 81-88. Washington, D.C.: The Catholic University of America, 2001.

Burrows, W. (Ed.). *Redemption and Dialogue: Reading Redemptoris Missio and Dialogue and Proclamation*. Maryknoll, NY: Orbis Books, 1994.

Capalla, F. "Interreligious Dialogue Should Be Mandatory Subject," *L'Osservatore Romano* 31:18 (May 6, 1998): 4-5.

Chang, A. "The Spirituality of Dialogue," *East Asian Pastoral Review* 19 (1982): 398-400.

Chia, E. (A) "The 'Absence of Jesus' in the VII FABC Plenary Assembly," *Vidyajyoti* 63 (1999): 892-899; **(B)** (Ed.). *Dialogue Resource Manual for Catholics in Asia*. Bangkok: FABC Office of Ecumenical and Interreligious Affairs, 2001; **(C)** "FABC's 'Response' to *Dominus Iesus*," *East Asian Pastoral Review* 38 (2001): 231-237; **(D)** "Towards an Interreligious Spirituality," *SEDOS Bulletin* 34 (2002): 232-239; **(E)** "Wanted: Interreligious Dialogue in Asia," *Studies in Interreligious Dialogue* 12 (2002): 101-110; **(F)** "FABC's Authority in Asia," *Vidyajyoti* 66 (2002):

992-1003; **(G)** "Thirty Years of FABC: History, Foundation, Context and Theology," *FABC Papers 106* (2003): 1-55.

D'Ambra, S. "Interreligious Dialogue in *Ecclesia in Asia*," In *The Future of the Asian Churches: The Asian Synod and Ecclesia in Asia*. **J. Kroeger** and **P. Phan** (Eds.), 110-114. Quezon City, Philippines: Claretian Publications, 2002.

D'Costa, G. **(A)** Theology and Religious Pluralism: *The Challenge of Other Religions*. Oxford: Basil Blackwell, 1986; **(B)** *Christian Uniqueness Reconsidered*. Maryknoll, NY: Orbis Books, 1990; **(C)** *The Meeting of Religions and the Trinity*. Maryknoll, NY: Orbis Books, 2000.

Degryse, O. *Interreligious Dialogue: The Asian Churches Set the Tone*. Louvain: Catholic University, 1999.

Dhavamony, M. **(A)** (Ed.). *Theology of Religions [Studia Missionalia* 42]. Rome: Editrice Pontificia Università Gregoriana, 1993; **(B)** *Ecumenical Theology of Religions*. Rome: Gregorian University Press, 2004.

Dupuis, J. **(A)** *Jesus Christ at the Encounter of World Religions*. Maryknoll, NY: Orbis Books, 1991; **(B)** "FABC Focus on the Church's Evangelizing Mission in Asia Today," *Vidyajyoti* 56 (1992): 449-468; similar presentation in: *FABC Papers 64* (1992): 1-19; **(C)** "The Church, the Reign of God and the 'Others'," *FABC Papers 67* (1993): 1-30; **(D)** *Toward a Christian Theology of Religious Pluralism*. Maryknoll, NY: Orbis Books, 1997; **(E)** *Christ and the Religions: From Confrontation to Dialogue*. Maryknoll, NY: Orbis Books, 2002; **(F)** "The Church's Evangelizing Mission in the Context of Religious Pluralism," *The Pastoral Review* 1 (2005): 20-31.

Evers, G. **(A)** (Ed.). *Bibliography on Interreligious Dialogue [Theology in Context Supplements* 7]. Aachen, Germany: Institute of Missiology, 1992; **(B)** *The Churches in Asia*. Delhi: ISPCK, 2005.

FABC and **CCA** (Federation of Asian Bishops' Conferences and Christian Conferences of Asia). *"Living and Working Together with Sisters and Brothers of Other Faiths: An Ecumenical Consultation," FABC Papers 49* (1987): 1-62.

FABC:TAC (Federation of Asian Bishops' Conferences: Theological Advisory Commission). **(A)** "Theses on Interreligious Dialogue" In *Being Church in Asia*. **J. Gnanapiragasam** and **F. Wilfred** (Eds.)., 7-28. Quezon City, Philippines: Claretian Publications, 1994 and *FABC Papers 48* (1987): 1-22; **(B)** "Asian Christian Perspectives on Harmony," *FABC Papers 75* (1996): 1-66 and *For All the Peoples of Asia II*, 229-298.

Fernando, L. "CBCI and FABC on Religious Pluralism," *Vidyajyoti* 64 (2000): 857-869.

Fitzgerald, M. (A) "Other Religions in the Catechism of the Catholic Church," *Islamochristiana* 19 (1993): 29-41; **(B)** "The Spirituality of Interreligious Dialogue," *Origins* 28:36 (February 25, 1999): 631-633; **(C)** "Pope John Paul II and Interreligious Dialogue: A Catholic Assessment," In *John Paul II and Interreligious Dialogue*. **B. Sherwin** and **H. Kasimov** (Eds.)., 207-220. Maryknoll, NY: Orbis Books, 1999.

Gioia, F. (Ed). *Interreligious Dialogue: The Official Teaching of the Catholic Church (1963-1995)*. Boston: Pauline Books and Media, 1997.

Gnanapiragasam, J. and **F. Wilfred.** (Eds.). *Being Church in Asia: Theological Advisory Commission Documents (1986-92)*. Quezon City, Philippines: Claretian Publications, 1994.

International Theological Commission (ITC). "Christianity and World Religions," *Origins* 27:10 (August 14, 1997): 149, 151-166.

Jadot, J. "The Growth in Roman Catholic Commitment to

Interreligious Dialogue since Vatican II," *Journal of Ecumenical Studies* 20 (1983): 365-378.

John Paul II. **(A)** "The Meaning of the Assisi Day of Prayer," *Origins* 16:31 (January 15, 1987): 561-563; **(B)** "The Spirituality of Interreligious Dialogue," *Origins* 31:24 (November 22, 2001): 404-405.

Kasper, W. "Relating Christ's Universality to Interreligious Dialogue," *Origins* 30:21 (November 2, 2000): 321, 323-327.

Knitter, P. **(A)** *One Earth, Many Religions: Multifaith Dialogue and Global Responsibility.* Maryknoll, NY: Orbis Books, 1995; **(B)** *Jesus and the Other Names: Christian Mission and Global Responsibility.* Maryknoll, NY: Orbis Books, 1996; **(C)** *Introducing Theologies of Religions.* Maryknoll, NY: Orbis Books, 2002.

Kroeger, J. **(A)** "The Commitment of Mission Societies in Asia to Interreligious Dialogue," *East Asian Pastoral Review* 26 (1989): 266-275; **(B)** *Interreligious Dialogue: Catholic Perspectives.* Davao City, Philippines: Mission Studies Institute, 1990; **(C)** "Cruciform Dialogue in Mission," *Bulletin: Pontificium Consilium pro Dialogo Inter Religiones* 28 (1993): 147-152; **(D)** "Bridging Interreligious Dialogue and Conversion," *Review for Religious* 55 (1996): 46-54; **(E)** "Missionary Work in Asia: Evangelization through Dialogue," *Catholic International* 7 (1996): 421-423; **(F)** "Milestones in Interreligious Dialogue," *Review for Religious* 56 (1997): 268-276; **(G)** *The Future of the Asian Churches* [Edited with **P. Phan**]. Quezon City: Claretian Publications, 2002; **(H)** "A Church Walking in Dialogue: Interreligious Dialogue Milestones," in: *Becoming Local Church*, 87-107, Quezon City, Philippines: Claretian Publications, 2003; similar presentation in *FABC Papers 107* (2003): 23-39; **(I)** (Ed.). "The Second Vatican Council and the Church in Asia: Readings and Reflections." *FABC Papers 117* (2006): 1-127; **(J)** *Theology from the Heart of Asia: FABC Doctoral Dissertations I-II.* Quezon City, Philippines: Claretian

Publications, 2008; **(K)** "Dialogue: Interpretive Key for the Life of the Church in Asia," *FABC Papers 130* (2010): 1-66.

Kung, H. **(A)** *Christianity and World Religions: Paths to Dialogue.* Maryknoll, NY: Orbis Books, 1986; **(B)** *Tracing the Way: Spiritual Dimensions of the World Religions.* New York: Continuum, 2002.

LaRousse, W. "Dialogue in the Teaching of the Asian Church," in: *Walking Together, Seeking Peace*, 309-324, Quezon City, Philippines: Claretian Publications, 2001.

Machado, F. **(A)** "Theology of Religions: A Reflection from a Catholic Point of View," *Vidyajyoti* 64 (2000): 727-742; **(B)** *"Dialogue and Mission*: A Reading of a Document of the Pontifical Council for Interreligious Dialogue," In *Milestones in Interreligious Dialogue*, C. Isizoh (Ed.)., 170-182. Rome/ Lagos: Ceedee Publications, 2002.

Menamparampil, T. "Pastoral Attention to Traditional Religions—Asia Perspective," In *Milestones in Interreligious Dialogue*, C. Isizoh (Ed.)., 341-349. Rome/Lagos: Ceedee Publications, 2002.

Mendoza, R. (A) "'Ray of Truth That Enlightens All': *Nostra Aetate* and Its Reception by the FABC," *Studies in Interreligious Dialogue* 16 (2006): 148-172; **(B)** *A Church in Dialogue with Peoples of Other Faiths: A Journey to the Kingdom in the Spirit (The Federation of Asian Bishops' Conferences: 1970-2007).* Doctoral Dissertation. Leuven: Catholic University of Leuven, Faculty of Theology, 2008.

Michel, T. **(A)** "Interreligious Dialogue in the Context of the Asian Synod," In *A Church on the Threshold.* **M. Seigel** (Ed.)., 3-14. Rome: SEDOS, 1998; **(B)** "A Variety of Approaches to Interfaith Dialogue," *Encounter: Documents for Muslim-Christian Understanding* 249 (1998): 3-9.

Painadath, S. "Theological Perspectives of FABC on Interreligious Dialogue," *Jeevadhara* 27 (1997): 272-288.

Pandiappallil, J. *Jesus the Christ and Religious Pluralism.* New York: The Crossroad Publishing Company, 2001.

Pathil, K. "New Ways of Being Church in Asia," *Third Millennium* 1 (1998): 4-19.

Paul VI. *Ecclesiam Suam. The Pope Speaks* 10 (1964-1965): 253-292.

Phan, P. (A) "Doing Theology in the Context of Cultural and Religious Pluralism: An Asian Perspective," *Louvain Studies* 27 (2002): 39-68; **(B)** *Being Religious Interreligiously: Asian Perspectives on Interfaith Dialogue.* Maryknoll, NY: Orbis Books, 2004.

Pieris, A. "An Asian Paradigm: Interreligious Dialogue and Theology of Religions," *The Month* 26 (1993): 129-134; similar presentation in *Fire and Water: Basic Issues in Asian Buddhism and Christianity.* 154-161, Maryknoll, NY: Orbis Books, 1996.

Pontifical Council for Interreligious Dialogue (PCID). **(A)** "The Attitude of the Church Towards the Followers of Other Religions: Reflections and Orientations on Mission and Dialogue," *L'Osservatore Romano* 17:26 (June 25, 1984): 10-11; **(B)** "Dialogue and Proclamation: Reflections and Orientations on Interreligious Dialogue and the Proclamation of the Gospel of Jesus Christ," Vatican City: PCID, 1991; **(C)** *Towards a Culture of Dialogue.* Vatican City: PCID, 1999; **(D)** *Meeting in Friendship.* Vatican City: PCID, 2000; **(E)** *Peace: A Single Goal and a Shared Intention.* Vatican City: PCID, 2002.

Poulet-Mathis, A. "Ecumenical and Interreligious Dialogue in Asia: Concerns and Initiatives of the Federation of Asian Bishops' Conferences," In *Mission and Dialogue: Theory and Practice.* **L. Mercado** and **J. Knight** (Eds.)., 63-93. Manila:

Divine Word Publications, 1989; similar presentation in *FABC Papers 49* (1987): 10-28.

Sherwin, B. and **H. Kasimow** (Eds.). *John Paul II and Interreligious Dialogue.* Maryknoll, NY: Orbis Books, 1999.

Sinaga, A. "Interreligious Endeavors within the FABC," In *A Church on the Threshold.* **M. Seigel**, (Ed.)., 72-82. Rome: SEDOS, 1998.

Sottocornola, F. "The Apostolic Exhortation *Ecclesia in Asia* and Interreligious Dialogue," In *Milestones in Interreligious Dialogue.* **C. Isizoh** (Ed.)., 255-267. Rome/Lagos: Ceedee Publications, 2002.

Swidler, L. (A) "The Dialogue Decalogue: Ground Rules for Interreligious Dialogue," *Horizons* 10 (1983): 348-351; **(B)** "Interreligious Dialogue: A Christian Necessity," *Cross Currents* 35 (1985): 129-147.

Tan, J. (A) "Theologizing at the Service of Life," *Gregorianum* 81 (2000): 541-575; similar presentation in *FABC Papers 108* (2003): 1-34; **(B)** "*Missio Inter Gentes*: Towards a New Paradigm in the Mission Theology of the Federation of Asian Bishops' Conferences (FABC)," *Mission Studies* (Leiden) 21 (2004): 65-95; similar presentations in *FABC Papers 109* (2004): 1-38; in Spanish in *Misiónes Extranjeras* 204 (2005): 5-30; in French and English in *Mission* (Canada) 12 (2005): 99-128, 129-155.

Thangaraj, M. *Relating to People of Other Religions: What Every Christian Needs to Know.* Nashville, Tennessee: Abingdon Press, 1997.

Thoppil, J. *Towards an Asian Ecclesiology: The Understanding of the Church in the Documents of the Federation of Asian Bishops' Conferences (1970-2000).* Shillong, India: Oriens Publications and Bangalore, India: Asian Trading Corporation, 2005.

Tirimanna, V. **(A)** "Theologizing in Asia: Pluralism, Relativism and Subjectivism," *Asia Journal of Theology* 14 (2000): 57-67; **(B)** (Ed.). *Sprouts of Theology from the Asian Soil: Collection of TAC and OTC Documents.* Bangalore: Claretian Publications, 2007.

Vadakumpadan, P. "Evangelisation in the Context of Non-Christian Religions," In *Missionaries of Christ*, 199-213. Shillong, India: Verdrame Institute Publications, 2006.

Wilfred, F. **(A)** "Dialogue Gasping for Breath? Towards New Frontiers in Interreligious Dialogue," *FABC Papers 49* (1987): 32-52; **(B)** "The Federation of Asian Bishops' Conferences (FABC): Orientations, Challenges and Impact," In *For All the Peoples of Asia I.* **G. Rosales** and **C. Arévalo** (Eds.)., xxiii-xxx. Quezon City, Philippines: Claretian Publications and Maryknoll, NY: Orbis Books, 1992; similar presentation in *FABC Papers 69* (1995): 1-10; **(C)** Jesus Christ in Today's Asia: An Interpretation of FABC Documents," In *From the Dusty Soil*, 161-175. Madras: University of Madras, 1995; **(D)** "What the Spirit Says to the Churches (Rev. 2:7)" [various editors], *Vidyajyoti* 62 (1998): 124-133.

World Council of Churches. "Guidelines for Dialogue and Relations with People of Other Religions," *Current Dialogue* 40 (2002): 16-21.

Zago, M. **(A)** "Dialogue in the Mission of the Churches of Asia—Theological Bases and Pastoral Perspectives," *East Asian Pastoral Review* 19 (1982): 388-397; similar presentation in *Kerygma* 17 (1983): 185-206; **(B)** "Interreligious Dialogue," In *Following Christ in Mission*, **S. Karotemprel** *et al.* (Eds.). 101-109. Pasay City, Philippines: Paulines Publications, 1996; **(C)** "The Spirituality of Dialogue," *Pro Dialogo* 101 (1999): 233-247.

TO LIVE IS TO EVANGELIZE
Recent Popes and Integral Evangelization

Evangelization, for many Catholics—both in Asia and worldwide, is a generally unfamiliar and relatively new term; recently has it been gaining wider recognition and acceptance. The Second Vatican Council as well as recent popes has placed evangelization at the center of the Church's identity and mission. The goal of this presentation is to focus specifically on the unique contributions of Paul VI and John Paul II to the understanding of evangelization in all of its rich, complex, multi-faceted, and interrelated dimensions. Pope Benedict XVI did not issue a specific document on missionary evangelization, while Paul VI penned *Evangelii Nuntiandi* (1975), and John Paul II issued *Redemptoris Missio* (1990). Succinctly stated, this piece will explore evangelization viewed holistically and integrally in the five-decade Vatican II era.

The word "evangelization" does not occur in the New Testament; however, *euaggelion* meaning "gospel" or "good news" occurs 72 times, 54 of which are in the Pauline corpus. It has a wide range on meanings: the whole Christian message (Mk 1:1); the good news of Jesus (II Cor 4:4); it is for all (Mk 13:10; 16:15); it is a revelation of God (Gal 1:11-12) which is to be believed (Mk 1:15) and proclaimed (I Cor 9:14, 16, 18). One must risk all for the gospel (Mk 8:35; Rom 1:16), serve it (Rom 1:1; 15:16), defend it (Phil 1:7, 16). *Euaggelion* is the good news of truth (Gal 2:5, 14), of hope (Col 1:23), of peace (Eph 6:15), of immortality (II Tim 1:10), of the risen Christ (I Cor 15:1ff; II Tim 2:8), and of salvation (Eph 1:13).

Vatican II speaks of mission and evangelization in a variety of contexts, The Decree on Missions (*Ad Gentes*) is replete with references: "the specific purpose of missionary activity is evangelization and the planting of the Church" (6); "the Church has the obligation and the sacred right to evangelize" (7); catechists have an important task to evangelize (17), as do the laity (21); the call to evangelize arises from a charism of the Spirit (23); various roles are fulfilled by missionary institutes (27), Propaganda Fidei (29), the people of God (35, 36), bishops and priests (38), religious institutes (40), and young Churches (*Lumen Gentium* 17). The Council asserts that it is especially the bishops' task to promote evangelization by the faithful (*Christus Dominus* 6); it is associated with the mission of the laity (*Apostolicam Actuositatem* 2, 6, 20, 26; LG 35). Priests are to learn the methods of evangelization (*Presbyterorum Ordinis* 19). The Eucharist is the source and summit of all evangelization (PO 5).

Following upon foundations in Sacred Scripture and in the documents of Vatican II, the pivotal contribution of Paul VI and John Paul II has been to locate evangelization on "center-stage" in describing the Church's contemporary mission. An obvious question arises: How does one capture the rich thought of these two popes? This author takes the path of an extensive presentation of the seminal document of each pope on the subject of evangelization. Thus, this presentation unfolds in three lengthy interrelated sections: Paul VI and *Evangelii Nuntiandi*, John Paul II and *Redemptoris Missio*, and a final synthetic overview of Integral Evangelization.

Paul VI and *Evangelii Nuntiandi*

Pope Paul VI (1963-1978) will always be remembered as a modern missionary pope; he made missionary journeys to all continents; he authored *Evangelii Nuntiandi* (EN), which became the *magna carta* for Catholic evangelization in the last quarter of the second millennium of Christianity. Without doubt, EN is one of the most important ecclesial documents of the post-Vatican II era. It presents a concise, inspiring, and programmatic challenge for the Church to enthusiastically engage in her God-given mission to preach the Gospel to the contemporary world—to living peoples, with their aspirations and anxieties, their cultures and religions, their hopes and conflicts. EN boldly addresses the topic of evangelization in the modern world.

Background. EN, a document of 23,000 words, was issued on December 8, 1975; it emerged from several rich sources and antecedents. Very few recent papal documents have been prepared with so much prior consultation with so many different sections of the Church over so long a time period. To understand the context and content of EN, it is necessary to examine the events surrounding the 1974 International Synod on Evangelization (Paul VI explicitly refers to the Synod over 30 times in EN).

The Synod (September 27-October 26, 1974) brought together over 200 bishops from all parts of the world, along with some priests, religious, and laity in a consultative capacity. Three full years had been devoted to preparations on local, national, and continental levels. Pastoral experiences and approaches to evangelization were widely shared; the method was decidedly an inductive (not deductive) approach. The Churches in the so-called Third World devoted much effort and enthusiasm to the process. One fine example was the dedicated commitment of the Federation of Asian Bishops' Conferences (FABC); their First Plenary Assembly (April 1974: Taipei, Taiwan) produced the insightful document: *Evangelization in Modern Day Asia*.

When the 209 bishops arrived in Rome in late 1974, they were well prepared, ready and enthusiastic to engage in the Synod's work. Pope Paul VI opened the Synod with a Eucharist celebrated in the Sistine chapel; he also delivered an opening address, encouraging frank discussion and honest exchange on the burning issues surrounding evangelization. Paul VI had set the stage; he faithfully attended all the general assemblies as a silent but attentive listener.

The Synod proceeded according to its three planned stages:

(a) *communication of pastoral experiences*; these included five continental reports and about 175 speeches of Synod Fathers; (b) *reflection on interrelated theological themes*; an attempt was made to integrate theological elements and pastoral experiences; it met difficulties and revealed many lacunae; (c) *preparation of conclusions*; working with an immense amount of material and items prepared by D. Grasso, C. Wojtyla, and D. S. Amalorpavadass, a drafting committee prepared a 41-page text.

On October 22 (just four days before the Synod's conclusion) three-quarters of the text was rejected; it had failed to capture the testimonies and insights, the searchings and propositions that characterized the first three weeks of Synod work. Thus, the final session of the Synod (October 26, 1974) was awaited with keen interest. Pope Paul VI addressed the assembly frankly and openly: "the synod of bishops has ended.... We should want to assess its achievements.... We cannot but be genuinely satisfied and optimistic about its outcome."

The pope continued: "The theme [of evangelization] is too wide and complex to be dealt with properly in so short a time or to yield all the conclusions to which its discussion might give rise. However, this Synod did again make the following contribution to the Church in our day: it enabled the voices of the local churches to be heard; it facilitated a better diagnosis of the current situation and a delineation of the principal elements of evangelization; it set in train the discussion of the practice and theory of evangelization in our time. For this reason we judge that the Synod as a whole has been fruitful. For it places at the disposal of Peter's successor, for the benefit of the entire Church, an abundance of advice, admonitions and proposals."

***Evangelii Nuntiandi* Emerges.** During a year-long gestation period, Pope Paul VI labored to produce from the rich experience and insights of the Synod a document that is clearly the work of discernment and synthesis. EN is at once synodal and papal and therefore deeply collegial. EN is structured in seven thematic chapters and framed with an introduction and conclusion. Chapter titles clearly indicate specific content (e.g. "What is Evangelization?" "The Methods of Evangelization"). The five-paragraph introduction contains several interpretive keys to the document.

Paul VI clearly saw his role in shaping EN to be part of his papal responsibility of "encouraging our brethren in their mission as evangelizers"; this task became for him "a daily preoccupation ... and a fundamental commitment of our Pontificate" (1). What emerged as EN had been described as Paul VI's "last and finest apostolic exhortation, a novel and effective form of the magisterium."

Secondly, EN was not written as a tightly reasoned and carefully nuanced theological treatise (although excellent theological reflection pervades the document). Paul VI notes that his words are designed to be a "meditation on evangelization"; he hopes that they will succeed "in inviting the whole People of God assembled in the Church to make the same meditation" (5). The pope returns to the theme of meditation throughout EN (cf. 40, 76). It is this very personal, even conversational, style of meditative reflection and exhortation that many have found attractive; it invites a frequent return to EN—even nearly 40 years later. It encourages personal reception and assimilation of the message; it exudes a poetic quality.

Paul VI notes that three key elements converge to highlight the importance of the promulgation of EN (2): the conclusion of the Holy Year (a special time of renewal); the tenth anniversary of the close of Vatican II (renewing the Church for mission); and, the first anniversary of the 1974 Synod. The pope again alludes to these anniversaries in the conclusion of EN, adding that the Church stands at "the eve of a new century, the eve also of the third millennium of Christianity" (81). Clearly, Paul VI wishes to focus the entire attention of the Church on the centrality of evangelization. He wishes to launch "a new period of evangelization" (2) so that Christ's followers "can bring the Christian message to modern man" (3) "with ever increasing love, zeal and joy" (1). Fulfillment of this task is for the pope, "our heartfelt plea" (81).

Three leitmotifs of EN have already been mentioned: the papal commitment to evangelization, the role of meditation, and the centrality of evangelization in the life of the Church. A fourth theme centers on fidelity, a double fidelity—to God's message and to people (cf. 4, 39, 63). This fidelity is "the central axis of evangelization" (4). In numerous places throughout EN, Paul VI carefully defines, nuances, and balances diverse elements within the evangelization process (e.g. local and universal Church, culture and faith, liberation and evangelization, strengths and limitations of popular religiosity, etc.). It is the unique genius of Paul VI to have achieved integration and balance on so many topics. Thus, *Evangelii Nuntiandi* prolongs the reflection on evangelization begun in the 1974 Synod and makes its insights available to the entire Church. Paul VI has gifted the Church with an inspirational and pastoral handbook for modern missionary activity.

Describing Evangelization. The understanding of the term "evangelization" found in EN reflects a comprehensive and inclusive view; its use may be described as an "umbrella concept." This broad and holistic view respects the fullness and complexity of the evangelizing process, aiming to achieve *effective* evangelization.

Sections 17 and 24 provide a long list of the various elements comprising the evangelizing action of the Church. Both sections also strongly insist upon integrating and balancing all facets of evangelization. "Any partial and fragmentary definition which attempts to render the reality of evangelization in all its richness, complexity and dynamism does so only at the risk of impoverishing it and even distorting it" (17). "Evangelization, as we have said, is a complex process made up of varied elements; ... they are complementary and mutually enriching" (24).

Paul VI explicitly notes that the Synod constantly challenged the Church "to relate these elements rather than to place them in opposition one to the other, in order to reach a full understanding of the Church's evangelizing activity" (24). The pope has, in fact, set forth in EN a comprehensive presentation which in later years has become widely accepted in the Church; it is diversely termed "integral / holistic" and coupled with "evangelization / liberation / salvation."

Note the broad and inclusive manner in which Paul VI speaks: "evangelizing means bringing the Good News into all the strata of humanity" (18); "upsetting, through the power of the Gospel, mankind's criteria of judgment" (19); "what matters is to evangelize man's culture and cultures" (20) so as to overcome "the split between the Gospel and culture [which] is without doubt the drama of our time" (20). The scope of evangelization extends to the full transformation of humanity and cultures in the light of the Gospel. Additional examples from the pope's writings could be mentioned, all illustrating Paul VI's broad and holistic view of evangelization. Here, then, is a key, a helpful category, a foundational insight, for an integrated interpretation of the entire text of EN.

Theological Foundations. Viewing evangelization holistically and integrally has important practical and pastoral ramifications. It allows Christians to appreciate the myriad manifestations of evangelization; individual gifts, talents, and charisms are desired and treasured (66); no individual or group is master of evangelization (15, 78); everyone acts "in communion with the Church" (60); "the work of evangelization is a basic duty of the People of God" (59).

These practical and pastoral dimensions of an integral approach to evangelization have as their basis solid theological foundations. They are anchored in "the Father's love" (26), in the entire life, mission, practice, and witness of Jesus, "the first evangelizer" (7, cf. 6-12). The Church "is born of the evangelizing activity of Jesus and the Twelve"; she "in her turn is sent by Jesus" (15). In the power of the Spirit, "the Apostles depart to all the ends of the earth in order to begin the great work of the Church's evangelization" (75). A brief look at the footnote references of the first two chapters of EN reveals how closely these theological foundations are linked with Sacred Scripture and the documents of the Second Vatican Council.

EN contains several beautiful descriptions of the Church as an evangelizing community. "Evangelization is in fact the grace and vocation proper to the Church, her deepest identity. She exists in order to evangelize"; "evangelizing all people constitutes the essential mission of the Church" (14). "The Church is an evangelizer, but she begins by being evangelized herself" (15).

Paul VI makes an important clarification in the first section of Chapter III: "The Content of Evangelization." He speaks of the distinction between the *essential* elements and the "living substance" of the Gospel message, and the *secondary* elements "whose presentation depends greatly on changing situations" (25). Within an integral view of evangelization, one must have a clear mind on the vital substance (26-28) in relation to the secondary aspects (29-39). Once again, the principle of "double fidelity" (4) enters; "evangelization would not be complete if it did not take account of the unceasing interplay of the Gospel and of man's concrete life, both personal and social" (29). In the mind of Paul VI, this continued nuancing and balanced integration are certainly part of the "drama of fidelity" (39).

Diverse Synod Themes. It has been noted that the 1974 Synod on Evangelization ended inconclusively and that the entire documentation of the proceedings was left in the pope's hands. EN reveals how Paul VI, not wishing the material to be lost, reworked many of the Synod's major themes into a stirring and unified presentation.

He addresses several questions in the mode of a pastoral synthesis: salvation and liberation (9, 27, 30-38), non-Christian religions (53, 80), religious liberty (39, 80), secularization (55), secularism (55-56), atheism (54-56), ecumenism (54, 76, 77), basic communities (58), diversified ministries (73), popular piety (48), sacraments in evangelization (23, 28, 47, 68), mass media (45, 80), Church as sign and sacrament of salvation (23, 59), violence (37), signs of the times (75-76), the local-universal Church dynamic (60-68), culture (20, 58), and the role of the Holy Spirit (75, 82).

Many of these diverse topics had been identified by Paul VI in his final Synod speech as areas of evangelization needing to be "better defined, nuanced, completed and subjected to further study." Commentators have noted how closely certain passages in EN resemble the actual interventions made on the Synod floor. Thus, EN is a testimony that Paul VI was involved as an intent listener and learner at the Synod; then, through his papal "charism of discernment" he fashioned his insights and reflections into a personal and spiritual testament on evangelization. EN is the fruit of long and profound meditation; it nourishes the spiritual life.

Special Themes. This summary overview of the scope of evangelization found in EN presents only the highlights of this dense and rich document. Some special themes deserve additional comment.

EN is an important document in two ways for the emerging theology of the *local Church*. It presents a basically positive and firm link between the local and the universal Church. It also shows the importance that the local community and its personal witnesses have in the whole process of inculturated evangelization. Basic ecclesial communities (58) have enormous potential to manifest the missionary character of the Church.

EN contains few direct references to *the missions*, as they were traditionally known. Where do missionary societies and organizations find their place in the contemporary world? In the fifth chapter, three specific tasks are mentioned; missionaries are to: (a) proclaim the Gospel for the first time to peoples and lands where it has not been heard (51); (b) engage and interact with the faithful adherents of other religions (53);

and, (c) assist the young Churches and promote missionary consciousness within them (56, 58).

The treatment of *world religions* in EN is not sufficiently developed. This is remarkable in a document authored by Paul VI whose first encyclical *Ecclesiam Suam* was dedicated to the theme of dialogue and who established the Secretariat for non-Christians in 1964. Several reasons for respecting and esteeming these religions are mentioned (53), but there is no theological understanding of religions in EN (Are non-Christians saved *in* and *through* their religions? Can these faith-traditions be called "ways of salvation"?). The openness expressed at the Synod which affirmed the wide action of the Holy Spirit and expressed the desire for interreligious dialogue is not pursued or promoted in EN; the term "dialogue" is not found in all of EN. In any case, one can be grateful for the encouragement given to foster an open and respectful attitude towards the great religions of the world.

The role that EN assigns to the promotion of *justice and human liberation* within the Church's evangelizing mission is a curious one. Many helpful clarifications on the concept of liberation are presented (29-39). EN notes that "Between evangelization and human advancement—development and liberation—there are in fact profound links" (31). Yet, to say that liberation "is not foreign to evangelization" (30) seems restrictive; this stands in contrast to the 1971 Synod that declared justice to be "a constitutive dimension of the preaching of the Gospel."

Impact on the Church. The Synod and EN have profoundly influenced the Church; they provided the inspiration, emphasis, and methodology to place evangelization in center spotlight in the Church. National and continental Church gatherings were inspired by EN; "Evangelization at Present and in the Future of Latin America" (CELAM: Puebla, 1979) is only one of many examples.

EN influenced the methodology of subsequent synods (the

synod proper followed later by a post-synodal document) as well as their topics of discussion (e.g. catechesis, family, reconciliation, etc.). EN also affirmed key Vatican II documents (*Lumen Gentium*, *Gaudium et Spes*, and *Ad Gentes*) and promoted their reception and implementation in the Church.

The Synod and EN manifested the positive contribution of "third-world" local Churches; the benefits of an inductive, collegial, and reflective method of theologizing were highlighted. The emergence of a truly "world church" received forward impetus. Missionary journeys, begun by Paul VI, have become a common papal *modus operandi*.

The Church has renewed her commitment to being a community of disciples and evangelizers (13, 15, 21, 24, 59, 66, 80), filled with joy and enthusiasm (73, 80), eager to give authentic witness (41, 76), under the dynamic action of the Holy Spirit, the principal agent of evangelization (75) and guided by Mary, the Star of Evangelization (82).

John Paul II and *Redemptoris Missio*

Karol Jósef Wojtyla was elected pope on October 16, 1978 and took the name John Paul II. Under his leadership the papal ministry became focused on evangelization and global mission, as he traveled to numerous countries, strengthened local Christian communities, encountered the followers of other religions, spoke on the social teachings of the Church, canonized saints and honored blesseds, met with youth and government leaders. Pope John Paul II has asserted that the Second Vatican Council has set the direction for his papacy; he has enunciated a clear vision for the Church in the third Christian millennium.

Gift of a Mission Encyclical. John Paul II's eighth encyclical *Redemptoris Missio* (RM) was issued on December 7, 1990; it celebrates the twenty-fifth anniversary of Vatican II's Mission Decree *Ad Gentes* and the fifteenth anniversary of Paul

VI's *Evangelii Nuntiandi*. In RM, the pope sounds a clarion and urgent call to all Church sectors to renew their enthusiasm and commitment to evangelize the world. Composed of eight chapters plus an introduction (1-3) and conclusion (92), RM has a "doctrinal" section (4-30) and a "pastoral" section (31-91), respectively treating the "Why" and "How" of contemporary mission and evangelization.

John Paul II begins by stating his conviction about "the *urgency of missionary activity*, a subject to which I am devoting the present Encyclical" (1). The Pope asserts: "Missionary activity specifically directed *ad gentes* [to the nations] appears to be waning." This fact "must arouse concern among all who believe in Christ." Why? Because "in the Church's history, missionary drive has always been a sign of vitality, just as its lessening is a sign of a crisis of faith" (2).

The Pope urges a "fresh impulse to missionary activity," the deepening of "commitment of the particular churches," and the harnessing of "all of the Church's energies to a new evangelization" (2-3). In a word, the focus of John Paul II is direct and clear: "I wish to invite the Church to *renew her missionary commitment*" (2). All are invited to participate: "*Peoples everywhere, open the doors to Christ!*" (3).

Vision of Evangelization. What view of evangelization emerges from a comprehensive analysis of the encyclical? Repeatedly, the document speaks of mission, evangelization and salvation in a holistic fashion: "Jesus came to bring integral salvation, one which embraces the whole person" (11); "evangelical witness ... is directed towards integral human development" (42); "action on behalf of integral development and liberation ... is most urgently needed" (58).

Integral evangelization, as repeatedly affirmed in the encyclical (20, 41-60), reflects current missiological thought as well as recent magisterial teaching. As already noted, Paul VI in EN clearly encouraged Catholics to view evangelization holistically; the second chapter of EN speaks of the complexity of the evangelizing action and its various complementary and mutually enriching elements. RM echoes this vision: "Mission is a single but complex reality, and it develops in a variety of ways" (41). Again, "mission is one and undivided, having one origin and one final purpose; but within it, there are different tasks and kinds of activity" (31). This is the vision of evangelization that the pope consistently promotes throughout RM.

Foundational Mission Theology. RM clearly affirms the foundations of mission theology and the centrality and urgency of mission in the life of the Church. The years following the Second Vatican Council were a golden opportunity to explore and debate, renew and clarify the Church's mission; and, it is true that the Council "has already borne much fruit in the realm of missionary activity.... Above all, there is a new awareness that *missionary activity is a matter for all Christians*" (2). Yet, John Paul II also discerned a need to reaffirm diverse aspects of the Catholic Church's foundational theology of Christian mission and evangelization.

At least one third of the encyclical (three chapters out of eight) deals with theological questions. Chapter One includes core elements of the dogmatic theology of Revelation and Faith, Christology and Soteriology, as well as Ecclesiology and Missiology. Chapter Two focuses on biblical theology, particularly the Kingdom of God. And, to the delight of missiologists, Chapter Three is completely devoted to Pneumatology, examining the role of the Holy Spirit in the life of the Church and her evangelizing mission.

The following are key emphases in the opening chapter: (a) All mission is centered in God's wonderful, generous loving plan of salvation (*mysterion*), made known through Jesus and accepted in faith. Jesus is the "definitive self-revelation of God" and "the fundamental reason why the Church is missionary by her very nature" (5); (b) While affirming with the Scriptures (I Tim 2:4) the universality of salvation, "the Church believes that God has established Christ as the one mediator and that it has been established as the universal sacrament of salvation" (9);

(c) The Pope unhesitatingly reaffirms these basics of Church teaching, noting that *"Mission is an issue of faith"* (11).

The biblical theme of the Kingdom (*basileia*) is the integrating leitmotif of the second chapter. Preaching the Kingdom and promoting its values are the evangelizing tasks of the Church which is "effectively and concretely at the service of the Kingdom" (20). The encyclical offers clarity and interpretation on other dimensions of Kingdom theology: the Kingdom of God and the Christ-event are complementary proclamations (16); the Kingdom necessarily has a transcendent horizon (17); the Kingdom "cannot be detached either from Christ or from the Church" (18); theocentrism and ecclesiocentrism demand a nuanced critique consistent with Church teaching (17-18).

Currently, the theology of the Holy Spirit (pneumatology) is of particular interest to missiologists and missionaries alike. "The Holy Spirit is indeed the principal agent of the whole of the Church's mission of evangelization. The Holy Spirit's action is preeminent in mission *ad gentes*" (21). The Spirit's centrality is emphasized because the Holy Spirit's "presence and activity affect not only individuals but also society and history, peoples, cultures and religions" (28). Ask any missionary and you will receive an eloquent personal testimony of the presence and power of the Spirit active in peoples, cultures, and religions— renewing the face of the earth! The acts of today's apostles continuously write the gospel of the Holy Spirit!

Transmitting the Urgency of Mission. The English subtitle given to RM is: "On the Permanent Validity of the Church's Missionary Mandate." Thus, mission is always and everywhere essential; it is "not considered a marginal task for the Church but is situated at the center of her life, as a fundamental commitment of the whole People of God" (32). Mission is "the greatest and holiest duty of the Church" (63). The Pope's affirmations resonate throughout the work: "I have chosen to travel to the ends of the earth in order to show this missionary concern" (1); "mission *ad gentes* is still in its infancy" (40); "I see the dawning of a new missionary age" (92).

No one seeks to minimize the Pope's assertions about the centrality and urgency of missionary evangelization; however, it is a valid question to ask about strategies for implementation. Words of exhortation must give way to programs of concrete actualization. In the considered judgment of this author, the encyclical is strong on the why of mission, but is only moderately successful on the *how*. Mission animation—the *how* of mission—requires continued discussion. While it is best accomplished locally, within the local Church, one can highlight some creative suggestions found within RM.

The Christian family is a key and irreplaceable force in evangelization (42); this insight is consistent with the teaching of Vatican II which termed the family the "domestic church" (LG 11). Promoting Christian family life should redound to mission awareness and animation. Material and financial donations are gratefully received, yet families are challenged to offer "a special contribution to the missionary cause of the Church by fostering missionary vocations among their sons and daughters" (80).

John Paul challenges Christians: Do you wish to promote mission? True disciples are urged to "carry out a sincere review of their lives regarding their solidarity with the poor" (60). As followers of Jesus, "we should reassess our own way of living" (81); "Fight hunger by changing your lifestyle" (59); "We cannot preach conversion unless we ourselves are converted anew every day" (47).

The role of missionary institutes and societies is crucial in worldwide evangelization; missionaries themselves should continue their "radical and total self-giving," initiate "new and bold endeavors," and "not allow themselves to be daunted by doubts, misunderstanding, rejection or persecution" (66). Diocesan seminarians and priests "must have the mind and heart of missionaries" (67). The Church must seek to expand the spheres "in which lay people are present and active as missionaries" (72). Missionary dynamism should become contagious!

Youth involvement is essential to mission and evangelization. They should be offered opportunities to visit overseas missions, to meet and offer hospitality to non-Christians and migrants within their own country (82). The idealism of youth is a potential resource—their rejection of violence and war, their desire for freedom and justice, their rejection of racism and closed nationalism, their affirmation of the dignity and role of women (86). The vision of Charles de Foucauld (as a "universal brother") can fire the imagination of youth (89) can be a path toward missionary commitment.

Additional Major Emphases. In composing a popular overview of a papal encyclical one faces the challenge of providing a balanced presentation. This writer sees several other major emphases on evangelization within the work; he devotes a paragraph to each theme.

Around the world *local churches* are the central actors in mission today; all evangelization necessarily is harmoniously accomplished in, with, and through the local Church which is responsible for the totality of mission. This is a sea change in the dynamics of mission; both local Churches and missionaries alike must explore the ramifications of this new reality. Many leads are found in the encyclical (26, 30, 39, 48-52, 62-64, 71, 83-85, 92).

Authentic evangelization is a *freely-offered gift*, not an external imposition which violates human dignity and freedom. Or again, witnessing and proclaiming Christ are not at odds with people's dignity as persons or their freedom of conscience (7-8). Genuine mission does not restrict freedom, but rather seeks to advance it; RM is clear: "*The Church proposes; she imposes nothing*" (39).

The Church needs *missionary vocations*. Individuals who receive the permanent, life-long vocation to foreign, transcultural mission are a treasured resource of the Church. Their vocation is necessary for the Church (32); it is a unique calling (27, 65); it is the model of the Church's missionary commitment (66); it is to be assiduously cultivated (79, 84), particularly by mission institutes themselves (65-66).

The encyclical looks positively upon *interreligious dialogue*, devoting several sections to presenting it comprehensively (55-57). Interfaith dialogue "is part of the Church's evangelizing mission, ... is not in opposition to the mission *ad gentes*, ... [and] *does not dispense from evangelization.*" This same section (55) speaks of God's call to all peoples and his presence to them "of which their religions are the main and essential expression." The Church's reverence for the followers of other faiths and religions is clearly affirmed by the encyclical.

In RM *women* receive the Pope's praise and gratitude for their outstanding contribution to evangelization: "I extend a special word of appreciation to the missionary Religious sisters" (70); "How can we forget the important role played by women"? (71). "It is necessary to recognize—and it is a title of honor—that some Churches owe their origins to the activity of lay men and women missionaries" (71).

The process of *inculturation* and its relationship to mission receives extensive treatment (25, 52-54, 76). Authentic evangelization involves the Church in the inculturation process, an "intimate transformation of authentic cultural values through their integration in Christianity and the insertion of Christianity in the various human cultures." This task is never finished and today it encounters new challenges—especially in large cities, "where new customs and styles of living arise together with new forms of culture and communication" (37). Mission and inculturation demand fresh initiatives and creativity in the techtronic age of the megalopolis!

The entire final chapter of *Redemptoris Missio* treats *missionary spirituality* (87-91). Four elements characterize Jesus' disciples-become-missionary: the missionary is to be led by the Spirit, to live the mystery of Christ who himself was sent, to love the Church and humanity as Jesus did, and to desire the holiness of saints. In a word, mission spirituality is "a journey towards holiness" (90) and the success of renewing the urgency of the Church's missionary impulse "demands holy missionaries" (90).

Additional Precious Details. In a work as long as RM one expects to find several details that demand further reflection. This synthesis presentation takes note of five additional themes and their importance for evangelization.

The *personalist philosophy* and orientation of John Paul II is manifested throughout the work. The person is always central in evangelization and all mission apostolates: in work for justice (42), in fostering interreligious dialogue (55-57), in promoting development; the human person "is the principal agent of development, not money or technology" (58). In uniquely personalist terms, the missionary is described as "a person of the Beatitudes" (91) and it is personal love that is always "*the driving force of mission*" (60).

The encyclical profusely expresses the *Church's gratitude* to its missionaries (2, 57, 60, 70). The Church's theologians provide an important service to the cause of evangelization (36) and should promote the study of world religions and science of missiology (83). The Church needs a renewed commitment to ecumenism within mission (50).

In looking at today's world from the viewpoint of evangelization, the document distinguishes *three situations*: "non-Christian" peoples, Christians requiring pastoral care, and the so-called "post-Christians"; all require special approaches (32-34). Geographically, the Pope emphasizes the missionary demands within Asia (37, 55, 91).

Significant and surprising is the fact that *one unique quote* appears verbatim no less than three times in the text (6, 10, 28): "we are obliged to hold that the Holy Spirit offers everyone the possibility of sharing in the Paschal Mystery in a manner known to God." One cannot mistake the Pope's assertion that God's loving plan for salvation includes each and every person!

Evangelization as *"God's work"* (24) is clearly affirmed; it is based "not on human abilities but on the power of the Risen Lord" (23). Missionaries are conscious that they owe their faith and vocations "not to their own merits but to Christ's special grace" (11). They must believe that "it is not we who are the principal agents of the Church's mission, but Jesus Christ and his Spirit" (36). A missioner's faith journey "proceeds along *the path* already trodden by the Virgin Mary" (92).

Fifteen years earlier (1975) Paul VI wrote that "Modern man listens more willingly to witnesses than to teachers, and if he does listen to teachers, it is because they are witnesses" (EN 41). This passage is recalled in *Redemptoris Missio* (42). It must continue to remain a central focus if the Church wishes to respond "with generosity and holiness to the calls and challenges of our time" (92).

Synthesis Overview of Integral Evangelization

Without doubt, both Paul VI and John Paul II have gifted the Church with a rich understanding of the theology and praxis of evangelization. In presenting the vision of each pope, this piece has consciously limited itself to *one pivotal document* on mission and evangelization authored by each pope [elements from John Paul II's *Ecclesia in Asia* could have validly been included]. *Evangelii Nuntiandi* for Paul VI and *Redemptoris Missio* for John Paul II are each a microcosm of their understanding of missionary evangelization. This fact is borne out if one simply recalls the many facets of evangelization presented in each of the two previous sections. Can the discussion be taken further?

Additional insight can be drawn from two documents issued by the Secretariat for Non-Christians (founded in 1964 by Paul VI and renamed in 1988 the Pontifical Council for Interreligious Dialogue). On Pentecost Sunday, 1984, the Secretariat promulgated the document entitled: "The Attitude of the Church toward the Followers of Other Religions:

Reflections and Orientations on Dialogue and Mission" (DM). Hidden in this little-known work on the interrelationship between dialogue and mission is a pivotal statement. This source affirms that mission and evangelization are understood "in the consciousness of the Church as a single but complex and articulated reality" (13).

Later, on Pentecost Sunday, 1991, the Pontifical Council for Interreligious Dialogue in conjunction with the Congregation for the Evangelization of Peoples presented the document: "Dialogue and Proclamation: Reflections and Orientations on Interreligious Dialogue and the Proclamation of the Gospel of Jesus Christ" (DP). Once again, the evangelizing mission of the Church is understood as a "single but complex and articulated reality" (2).

Both documents emphasize the unity and integral nature of evangelization, while at the same time affirming that evangelization necessarily comprises many dimensions; it is a complex reality. In addition, this multi-faceted concept can be explained and articulated.

Naming the Elements. Despite the lengthy and complex titles of the 1984 and 1991 documents just mentioned, these two sources have added considerable clarity to a Catholic understanding of missionary evangelization. The clarity results from the fact that "principal elements" are specifically named. Thus, mission and evangelization are composed of: (a) presence and witness; (b) commitment to social development and human liberation; (c) liturgical life, prayer and contemplation; (d) interreligious dialogue; and, (e) proclamation and catechesis (cf. DM 13 and DP 2). In a word, the one evangelizing mission of the Church is comprised of several component elements and authentic forms. This is integral or holistic evangelization; this is—in compact expression—the wide view of evangelization promoted by Paul VI and John Paul II in EN and RM; it is also present in the apostolic exhortation of Pope Francis, *Evangelii Gaudium* (some apropos references will be supplied in the paragraphs below).

This five-point vision has served the Church well over the past decades; this approach takes the thought of two popes and two documents and expresses it in a manner that ordinary Catholics can readily grasp and appreciate. At the same time, it does not do violence to the richness and complexity of missionary evangelization. One easily perceives that the thought expressed in EN and RM is adequately captured in this five-point schema; in turn, employing this helpful schema enables a smooth maneuvering through lengthy papal documents. Viewing evangelization through its various essential dimensions results in clarity, insight, and proper integration. This is a Catholic vision of evangelization.

Exploring the Five Dimensions. Further insight into the integral nature of evangelization is attained by specifically relating the five principal elements with both papal documents (EN and RM). This exercise illustrates that "evangelizing means bring the Good News into all strata of humanity" (EN 18).

According to Paul VI, *Christian presence and witness of life* form the "initial act of evangelization" (EN 21). Daily activities, living together in harmony, lives as individuals of integrity, duties in the community—all these are to be a basic "faith-witness" that demonstrates how Christian living is shaped by Christian faith and values. Through this wordless witness, "Christians stir up irresistible questions in the hearts of those who see how they live" (EN 21). And, in today's world, people desire and respect authentic witnesses (cf. EN 41; RM 11, 42; EG 14, 20, 119-121, 149-151). In Asia, the late Mother Teresa of Calcutta, known for her loving and selfless care of the poorest of the poor, is an "icon" of Christian presence, life, and service (cf. EA 7).

Community living as good neighbors based on faith convictions should naturally issue in a *commitment to social development and human liberation*, a genuine service of humanity. This means serving the most unfortunate, witnessing to justice, defending the integrity of creation; this dimension of evangelization includes the whole area of social concerns, ranging from peace-building, education and health services to promoting family life and good government. The area of human development or human promotion is a vast area of the Church's evangelizing mission (cf. EN 18-19, 29-33; RM 58-60; EG 50-109, 181-185, 197-216).

All evangelizing activities are inserted into specific contexts; particularly in Asia, these activities naturally assume an interreligious dimension. Thus, the Church in Asia, similar to most places in the world of today, accomplishes her mission in pluralistic and diverse cultures; she enters into *interreligious dialogue*, cooperating with the followers of the great religious traditions. Interreligious dialogue takes many forms; there are the dialogues of daily life, deeds of service, religious experts, and faith experience, as well as other forms. John Paul II asserts: "Interreligious dialogue is a part of the Church's evangelizing mission" (RM 55). This dialogue emerges from one's faith convictions. In contemporary circumstances, particularly in Asia, dialogue with religions and cultures is the truly appropriate Christian response (cf. EN 20, 53; RM 52-54, 55-57; EG 115-118, 238-243, 250-254).

In mission today there is the role of *explicit Gospel proclamation and catechesis*. This dimension of evangelization includes preaching, catechesis on Christian life, teaching the content of the faith; in a word, this means "telling the Jesus story." When the Holy Spirit opens the door and when the time is opportune, Christians do tell the Jesus story, giving explicit witness and testimony to the faith. Others are invited, in freedom of conscience, to come to know, love and follow Jesus. Through proclamation Christians themselves are further instructed in their faith; this is the process through which the Christian faith is communicated to the next generation of believers (cf. EN 22, 27, 42; RM 44-51; EG 3, 12, 24, 110-111, 246).

Finally, integral evangelization and liberation will necessarily include *liturgical life, prayer and contemplation*. No one can effectively be engaged in the Church's mission without a strong faith and prayer-life. Evangelization needs holy men and women who are themselves on fire with the love of Christ; spreading the fire of the Gospel will be accomplished only by those already burning with an experience of Christ. Holiness is an irreplaceable condition for evangelizers. The "God-experience" achieved in prayer and contemplation, in sacramental and liturgical life, will illumine and transform all other dimensions of evangelization (cf. EN 23, 43-44, 47; RM 46-49, 87-92; EG 47, 173, 259-288).

Obviously, these five dimensions of an integral understanding of evangelization complement and reinforce each other. In speaking of the complexity of the Church's evangelizing action, Paul VI gave a timely admonition: "Any partial and fragmentary definition which attempts to render the reality of evangelization in all its richness, complexity and dynamism does so only at the risk of impoverishing it and even of distorting it." The pope continued: "It is impossible to grasp the concept of evangelization unless one tries to keep in view all its essential elements" (EN 17; cf EG 176).

Thus, an older concept of the Church's mission has been set aside. No longer are the elements of social justice, interfaith dialogue, peace-building, education and health care, life-witness, etc. simply "preparatory" to evangelization [*praeparatio evangelica*]; all five "principal elements" here described are constitutive of a holistic and integral understanding. Paul VI and John Paul II have expanded the horizons of evangelization; the more restrictive view, which held that only explicit Gospel proclamation and sacramental life constituted mission, has been superseded.

Concomitant with this expanded vision of evangelization, one finds a renewed emphasis on the missionary nature of the *entire Church* (cf. AG 2; EN 14, 59; RM 61-76; EG 14, 20, 119-121). Every baptized member of the Church is an evangelizer, whether layperson, ordained, or religious. Previously, when evangelization was linked more exclusively with explicit Gospel proclamation and sacramental life, laity often found it difficult to appreciate how they were to be evangelizers. Today, Catholic evangelization engages the entire Church (from top to bottom; especially, all the local churches), all states of life (lay, religious, ordained, married, single), all apostolic activities and forms of witness (the five principal elements—and other aspects). Yes, the totality of Christian missionary evangelization embraces all these dimensions.

Conclusion. This lengthy piece has attempted a panoramic overview of a Catholic vision of evangelization. Through a presentation of the vision of Paul VI and John Paul II in EN and RM (parts one and two), the bases for a renewed, holistic, and integral understanding of evangelization were established. The third and final part presented a focused synthesis, employing the five principal and constitutive elements of a Catholic vision of evangelization.

When many words have been uttered, when much ink has been spilt, when definitions and categories have been clarified, and when one more presentation has been completed, Catholic Christians must step back and radically affirm that: *All mission and evangelization is God's project. The Holy Spirit is always the principal agent of evangelization.* For evangelizers, missionaries, catechists, religious and lay alike, mission necessarily means trying to find out what God wills and what he is doing. Then, authentic evangelizers bend their wills to God's will, joyfully surrender to God's loving plan, and expend all efforts and energy to become worthy instruments that enable God's design to unfold. Evangelization, at heart and center, is an issue of faith (cf. RM 11). For Christians, for all local Churches, to live is to evangelize, to truly become "missionary disciples" (EG 120)!

RECENT POPES AND EVANGELIZATION
A Selected Bibliography

Amaladoss, M. "Evangelization in Asia: A New Focus?" In *Making All Things New: Dialogue, Pluralism and*

Evangelization in Asia, 103-120. Maryknoll, NY: Orbis Books, 1990.

Arévalo, C. (A) "The Church in Asia and Mission in the 1990s," *FABC Papers 57b*. Hong Kong: FABC Secretariat, 1990; **(B)** "Notes on the Apostolic Exhortation of Pope Paul VI, *Evangelii Nuntiandi*." In *Faith, Ideologies and Christian Options* [Loyola Papers 7/8], H. de la Costa *et al* (Eds.)., 38-60. Manila: Cardinal Bea Institute, 1976.

Bacani, T. (A) "The Need for a New Evangelization," *FABC Papers 66*: 11-25. Hong Kong: FABC Secretariat, 1993; **(B)** "The Renewed Integral Evangelization Envisioned by the Second Plenary Council of the Philippines," *Philippiniana Sacra* 28:83 (May-August, 1993): 311-320.

Burrows, W. (Ed.). *Redemption and Dialogue: Reading Redemptoris Missio and Dialogue and Proclamation*. Maryknoll, NY: Orbis Books, 1993.

Claver, F. "The Church in Asia Twenty and Forty Years after Vatican II: Personal Reflections: 1985 and 2005," In *Exploring the Treasures of Vatican II*. **J. Kroeger** (Ed.)., 119-135. Quezon City, Philippines: Claretian Publications and Jesuit Communications, 2011.

Degrijse, O. "John Paul II's Missionary Encyclical *Redemptoris Missio*: A Challenge for Missionary Institutes?" *Omnis Terra* 27:235 (February, 1993): 69-77 and 27:236 (March, 1993): 120-124.

Dorr, D. "*Redemptoris Missio*—Reflections on the Encyclical," *The Furrow* 42:6 (June, 1991): 339-347.

D'Souza, H. (A) "Pope John Paul II's New Challenge to Asia," *L'Osservatore Romano* 24:14 (April 8, 1991): 6, 8; **(B)** "*Redemptoris Missio* Confirms FABC Statements," *Asia Focus* 8:26 (July 10, 1992): 7.

Dulles, A. **(A)** "John Paul II and the New Evangelization," *America* 166:3 (February 1, 1992): 52-59, 69-72; **(B)** "Seven Essentials of Evangelization," *Origins* 25:23 (November 23, 1995): 397-400; **(C)** *Evangelization for the Third Millennium*. Mahweh, NJ: Paulist Press, 2009.

Dupuis, J. **(A)** "Apostolic Exhortation *Evangelii Nuntiandi* of Pope Paul VI," *Vidyajyoti* 40:5 (May, 1976): 218-230; **(B)** "FABC Focus on the Church's Evangelizing Mission in Asia Today," *Vidyajyoti* 56:9 (September, 1992): 449-468; **(C)** "Evangelization and Mission," In *Dictionary of Fundamental Theology*. **R. Latourelle** (Ed.)., 275-282. New York: Crossroad, 1995.

Falciola, P. *Evangelization according to the Mind of Paul VI*. Rome: Pontifical Missionary Union, 1982.

Fitzgerald, M. *"Evangelii Nuntiandi* and World Religions," *African Ecclesial Review* 21:1 (February, 1979): 34-43.

Flannery, A. (Ed.). *Evangelization Today*. Northport, NY: Costello Publishing Company, 1977.

Franciscus (Pope Francis). *Evangelii Gaudium* (*The Joy of the Gospel*). Rome: Vatican Press, 2013.

Gabriel, M. *John Paul II's Mission Theology in Asia: Agenda for the Third Millennium* (2d ed.). Mandaluyong City, Philippines: Academic Publishing Corporation, 1999 [Extensive Bibliography].

George, F. "One Lord and One Church for One World: The Tenth Anniversary of *Redemptoris Missio*," *L'Osservatore Romano* 34:5 (January 31, 2001): 7-10.

Giordano, P. "Towards Understanding the New or Integral Evangelization: The Visit of Pope John Paul II to the Philippines, January 12-16, 1995," *Timon* 2 (1994-1995): 1-18.

Greinacher, N. and **A. Müller** (Eds.). *Evangelization in the World Today*. New York: The Seabury Press, 1979.

John Paul II. *Redemptoris Missio*. In *The Pope Speaks* 36:2 (1991): 138-183; *Synthesis Text*: "Pope John Paul II's Gift." In *Living Mission: Challenges in Evangelization Today*, **J. Kroeger**. 141-159. Maryknoll, NY: Orbis Books and Quezon City, Philippines: Claretian Publications, 1994 and 2009.

Karotemprel, S. "*Redemptoris Missio* and Evangelization in Asia," *Indian Missiological Review* 14:3-4 (December, 1992): 28-33.

Keerankeri, G. "Many Expressions of One Mission," *Vidyajyoti* 57:3 (February, 1993): 128-132.

Kroeger, J. **(A)** *The Philippine Church and Evangelization: 1965-1984 [Human Promotion as an Integral Dimension of the Church's Mission of Evangelization: A Philippine Experience and Perspective since Vatican II - 1965-1984]*. Rome: Pontifical Gregorian University, 1985 [Extensive Bibliography]; **(B)** "Contemporary Mission in Asia," *The Japan Missionary Bulletin* 44:4 (Winter, 1990): 282-286; **(C)** "Rekindling Mission Vitality and Enthusiasm: *Redemptoris Missio* - A Commentary," *Indian Missiological Review* 14:3-4 (December, 1992): 15-22; **(D)** *Living Mission: Challenges in Evangelization Today*. Maryknoll, NY: Orbis Books and Manila, Philippines: Claretian Publications, 1994 and 2009; **(E)**"*Redemptoris Missio*," In *The Wojtyla Years* [*New Catholic Encyclopedia XX*]. **J. Komonchak** *et al*. (Eds.)., 231-232. Washington, DC: The Catholic University of America, 2001; reprinted in: *New Catholic Encyclopedia - Second Edition: XI*. **T. Carson** and **J. Cerrito** (Eds.)., 990-992. New York: Thomson-Gale, 2003.

Lopez-Gay, J. "Theological Aspects of the Apostolic Exhortation *Evangelii Nuntiandi*," *Omnis Terra* 11:82 (February, 1977): 167-179.

McCormack, W. (Ed.). *"To the Ends of the Earth"*:

Missionary Catechesis of Pope John Paul II. New York: Propagation of the Faith Publications, 1995.

McGregor, B. "Commentary on *Evangelii Nuntiandi*," *Doctrine and Life* 27:3-4 (March-April, 1977): 53-97.

Miller, J. *"Redemptoris Missio,"* In *The Encyclicals of John Paul II*. 478-570. Huntington, IN: Our Sunday Visitor, Inc., 1996 [Extensive Bibliography].

Müller, K. *et al.*, (Eds.). *Dictionary of Mission: Theology, History, Perspectives*. Maryknoll, NY: Orbis Books, 1997.

Neuner, J. "Mission in *Ad Gentes* and in *Redemptoris Missio*," *Vidyajyoti* 56:5 (May, 1992): 228-241.

Paul VI. *Evangelii Nuntiandi*. In *The Pope Speaks* 21:1 (1976): 4-51; *Synthesis Text*: "Pope Paul VI's Gift." In *Living Mission: Challenges in Evangelization Today*, **J. Kroeger.** 129-140. Maryknoll, NY: Orbis Books and Quezon City, Philippines: Claretian Publications, 1994 and 2009.

Phan, P. (Ed.). *The Asian Synod: Texts and Commentaries*. Maryknoll, NY: Orbis Books, 2002.

Piryns, E. "A New Approach to Mission and Evangelization," *Philippiniana Sacra* 30:88 (January-April, 1995): 81-98.

Quatra, M. *At the Side of the Multitudes*. Quezon City, Philippines: Claretian Publications, 2000.

Tan Yun-ka, J. *"Missio ad Gentes" in Asia: A Comparative Study of the Missiology of John Paul II and the Federation of Asian Bishops' Conferences*. Doctoral Thesis in Theology, Washington, DC: The Catholic University of America, 2002.

Vadakumpadan, P. *Evangelisation Today*. Shillong, India: Vendrame Missiological Institute [Sacred Heart College], 1989.

6

BECOMING MISSIONARY LOCAL CHURCHES
FABC Perspectives and Insights

The Church has joyfully celebrated the fiftieth anniversary of the beginning of the Second Vatican Council (1962-2012). In addition, the fiftieth year since the issuance of the Council's missionary decree *Ad Gentes* (December 7, 1965) approaches. One awaits the fortieth anniversary of Pope Paul VI's inspirational apostolic exhortation *Evangelii Nuntiandi* (December 8, 1975), as well as twenty-fifth anniversary of John Paul II's mission encyclical *Redemptoris Missio* (December 7, 1990). In this context, the local Churches in Asia continue to explore their understanding and commitment to the Church's mission of evangelization. The Christian communities of this vast continent seek to listen to "what the Spirit is saying to the Churches" (Rev. 2:7, 11, 17, 29; 3:6, 13, 22). They seek to follow Jesus, the first evangelizer and missionary of the Father, who took flesh as an Asian; the Savior of the world was born in Asia. With renewed zeal and vigor, Asia's Churches accept their missionary vocation; with John Paul II they hope and pray that "in the third Christian Millennium *a great harvest of faith* will be reaped in this vast and vital [Asian] continent" (*Ecclesia in Asia* 1).

This presentation explores the vision and some significant contributions of the Federation of Asian Bishops' Conferences (FABC) for the renewal of missionary evangelization in Asia extending over the lengthy experience following upon the Council; some auxiliary material is also drawn from *Ecclesia in Asia* (EA). After a very brief introduction to the FABC, this essay highlights areas where the Asian bishops have contributed to enabling the Churches of Asia to accomplish their mission of evangelization. Three themes will be unfolded: (a) FABC insights into the Theology of Local Church; (b) the FABC

"Pastoral Spiral" Methodology; and (c) some "Asian-born" Mission Initiatives emerging in the Vatican II era; treatment of the "Asian Theology of Local Church" will receive the most extensive presentation. Related topics would be: (a) the FABC Approach of Dialogue; (b) the Positive View of Religions promoted in Asia; and (c) a contemporary description of the Motives for Mission [these three topics are treated elsewhere]. This overview of the FABC contributions to the theology of Local Church and Mission enables one to validly assert that the FABC is truly "Asia's Continuing Vatican II."

An FABC Introduction. The Federation of Asian Bishops' Conferences (FABC) has been the most influential body in the Asian Church since the Vatican Council. FABC's roots are found in the 1970 meeting of 180 Asian bishops with Pope Paul VI in Manila; the FABC documents, spanning over four decades, are an essential source and wellspring for comprehending the dynamic development of mission, theology, dialogue, ecclesiology, and evangelization in Asia's local Churches. A Spirit-inspired instrument, the FABC has fostered the genuine local reception of the teachings of the Council, enabling them to be concretized for all the peoples of Asia.

The FABC, as described in a previous chapter, is a continent-wide episcopal structure that brings together fourteen bishops' conferences from the following countries as full members: Bangladesh, India, Indonesia, Japan, Korea, Laos-Cambodia, Malaysia-Singapore-Brunei, Myanmar (Burma), Pakistan, Philippines, Sri Lanka, Taiwan, Thailand, and Vietnam. FABC has eleven associate members drawn from the ecclesiastical jurisdictions of East Timor, Hong Kong, Kazakhstan, Kyrgyzstan, Macau, Mongolia, Nepal, Siberia, Tadjikistan, Turkmenistan, and Uzbekistan. Thus, in total, twenty-eight countries are represented in the FABC.

The FABC has a modest central structure; in addition, there are nine FABC offices, which carry out many concrete projects and initiatives. These offices, located in various Asian nations, are focused on evangelization, social communications, laity and family, human development, education and faith formation, ecumenical and interreligious affairs, theological concerns, clergy, and consecrated life. Each of these nine offices sponsors a wide variety of activities promoting the growth of the Asian local Churches. The offices of human development, evangelization, interreligious dialogue, and theological concerns have been particularly productive.

The supreme body of the FABC is the Plenary Assembly. Official delegates from member conferences and the FABC offices attend; there are many invited consultant participants. It is noteworthy that the "non-bishops" in attendance often reach nearly fifty percent of the total participants. Ten plenary assemblies, usually held every four years, have been convened, extending from 1974 to 2012. They have been held in: **I.** Taipei, Taiwan: 1974; **II.** Calcutta, India: 1978; **III.** Bangkok, Thailand: 1982; **IV.** Tokyo, Japan: 1986; **V.** Bandung, Indonesia: 1990; **VI.** Manila, Philippines: 1995; **VII.** Samphran, Thailand: 2000; **VIII.** Daejeon, Korea: 2004; **IX.** Manila, Philippines: 2009; and **X.** Xuan Loc and Ho Chi Minh City, Vietnam: 2012.

The FABC has promoted the bonds of communication among the bishops in the region and has contributed to the development of a shared vision about the Church and her evangelizing mission in Asia. The initial impetus for the FABC theological orientation was given by the first plenary assembly in 1974; for the Church in Asia to truly discover its own identity it must continually engage in a three-fold dialogue with the peoples (especially the poor), the cultures, and the religions of Asia. This programmatic vision has guided the FABC for four decades. Through the FABC, an ecclesiology and missiology of the Asian Churches has been shaped.

It remains true that, independent of size or numbers, each local Church is called to mission in the power of the Spirit. No Asian Church is so small or poor that it does not have something to give, and likewise, no Asian Church is so large and powerful that is does not have something to receive. A "new way of being Church" uniquely adapted to the Asian context and challenges has emerged. Indeed, the FABC has fostered an "Asian Pentecost"!

THEOLOGY OF LOCAL CHURCH AND MISSION

Explore any major document that has emerged from the extensive reflection of the FABC and you will probably find several creative insights on the local Church in the Asian context. Historically, it was the 1970 Asian pastoral visit of Pope Paul VI with the Asian bishops that gave the impetus for the local Churches to begin formulating a vision of Church and mission adequate to the "new world being born" in Asia in the post-colonial period. They asked themselves: How would local faith-communities respond to the grace that was the Second Vatican Council? How would the Churches incarnate a decisive "turning to history" and a "turning to the Gospel" within history "for all the peoples of Asia"? Consistent, prolonged, pastoral and theological reflection on the Church and her mission of evangelization has enabled the FABC to articulate an overall vision that captures what "being Church in Asia today" truly means. The insights have grown out of a belief that the Spirit was speaking to the Churches.

FABC pastoral-theological reflection is decidedly inductive— emerging from life's concrete realities. Therefore, an ecclesiology with local Church as its focal point most adequately captures the hopes and aspirations of local peoples. As the community of Jesus' disciples in Asia, the Church consistently links her identity with Asia's peoples and their life situations. She seeks to be—in fact, not only in theory—the "Church of the poor" and the "Church of the young." She shares the vicissitudes of the "Church of silence" in several parts of Asia. Her pastoral priorities concern the displaced (refugees and migrants), women and the girl-child, youth, families, the poor, the followers of Asia's great religious traditions. She actively fosters increasing communion among Asia's local Churches in unity with the See of Peter, which lovingly presides over the universal Church; she promotes authentic catholicity.

The theological thematic of *local Church* provides an appropriate, integrating center for the life of Asia's faith-communities. This fact helps explain why internationally some of the very best theological reflection on local Church has emerged in Asia and through the FABC. It is imperative to tell the story of local Church in Asian and FABC theological reflection—with all its depth, richness, and inspiration. Methodologically, this presentation of FABC material on the local Church is unfolded chronologically; the format lends itself to greater clarity. In addition, quoting the FABC materials directly and extensively avoids diluting the freshness, creativity, and insightfulness of the original documents.

FABC I. The First FABC Plenary Assembly in 1974 focused on the theme: "Evangelization in Modern Day Asia" (it was also a preparation for the Synod on Evangelization to be held in Rome later that same year). The Asian Churches through their bishops defined the central and most urgent mission duty incumbent upon them: "The primary focus of our task of evangelization then, at this time in our history, is the building up of a truly local church. For the local church is the realization and the enfleshment of the Body of Christ in a given people, a given place and time" (FABC I, 9-10).

"It is not a community in isolation from other communities of the Church one and catholic. Rather it seeks communion with all of them. With them it professes the one faith, shares the one Spirit and the one sacramental life. In a special way it rejoices in its communion and filial oneness with the See of Peter, which presides over the universal Church in love" (FABC I, 11).

"The local church is a church incarnate in a people, a church indigenous and inculturated. And this means concretely a church in continuous, humble and loving dialogue with the living traditions, the cultures, the religions—in brief, with all the life-realities of the people in whose midst it has sunk its roots deeply and whose history and life it gladly makes its own. It seeks to share in whatever truly belongs to that people: its meanings and its values, its aspirations, its thoughts and its language, its songs and its artistry. Even its frailties and failings it assumes, so that they too may be healed. For so did God's Son assume the totality of our fallen human condition (save only for sin) so that He might make it truly His own, and redeem it in His paschal mystery" (FABC I, 12).

Asian Colloquium on Ministries in the Church. Three years later in 1977, during the Asian Colloquium on Ministries in the Church (ACMC) held in Hong Kong, the theme of local church received another impetus: "… the decisive new phenomenon for Christianity in Asia will be the emergence of genuine Christian communities in Asia—Asian in their way of thinking, praying, living, communicating their own Christ-experience to others. The consequences will be tremendous not only for the ministries the Asian Churches will have to perform but also for all aspects of their life. We should beware of seeing our future mission in categories that belong to the past, when the West shaped the Churches' history. If the Asian Churches do not discover their own identity, they will have no future" (ACMC 14).

"Each local Church is determined by her human context and lives in a dialectical relationship with the human society into which she is inserted as the Gospel leaven…. Each local Church, in order to be viable, needs to become fully responsible and must have the legitimate autonomy which her natural and harmonious growth demands" (ACMC 25).

"Asian Churches then must become truly Asian in all things. The principle of indigenization and inculturation is at the very root of their coming into their own. The ministry of Asian Churches, if it is to be authentic, must be relevant to Asian societies. This calls on the part of the Churches for originality, creativity and inventiveness, for boldness and courage" (ACMC 26).

"Since Christ's mission is universal, all local Churches are called to live in communion with each other. This bond of unity, visibly expressed in the college of bishops presided over by the Bishop of Rome, implies that the search of each Church for ministries adapted to her needs is subject to verification and testing by the other Churches. In this bond of union lies the guarantee of the true apostolicity and catholicity of each local Church" (ACMC 27).

FABC II. The Second FABC Plenary Assembly in 1978 was organized around the theme: "Prayer—The Life of the Church of Asia." The Bishops-delegate noted that an important motive for their assembly was "to deepen our knowledge of our local churches" (FABC II, 1), and they addressed "the tasks which the carrying-out of the mission of the Church in Asia demands: commitment to the upbuilding of Asian communities in the life of the Gospel, to inculturation of Christian faith and life, to the endeavor for total human development and authentic liberation of peoples in justice and love, to interreligious dialogue and to renewed missionary formation" (FABC II, 3).

International Mission Congress. The successful International (though predominantly Asian) Mission Congress (IMC) held in 1979 in Manila once again strongly affirmed the centrality of the local Church for a "new age of mission" in Asia.

"What is the newness of this 'new age of mission'? First, the realization in practice that 'mission' is no longer, and can no longer be, a one-way movement from the 'older churches' to the 'younger churches,' from the churches of the old Christendom to the churches in the colonial lands. Now—as Vatican II already affirmed with all clarity and force—every local church is and cannot be but missionary. Every local church is 'sent' by Christ and the Father to bring the Gospel to its surrounding milieu, and to bear it also into all the world. For every local church this is a *primary task*. Hence we are moving beyond both the vocabulary and the idea of 'sending churches' and 'receiving churches,' for as living communities of the one Church of Jesus Christ, every local church must be a sending church, and every local church (because it is not on earth ever a total realization of the Church) must also be a receiving church. Every local church is responsible for its mission, and co-responsible for the mission of all its sister-churches. Every local church, according to its possibilities, must share whatever its gifts are, for the needs of other churches, for mission throughout [hu]mankind, for the life of the world" (IMC 14).

"Once again, what is the newness of this 'new age of mission'? We believe that the Spirit of the Lord calls each people and each culture to its own fresh and creative response to the Gospel. Each local church has its own vocation in the one history of salvation, in the one Church of Christ. In each local church, each people's history, each people's culture, meanings and values, each people's traditions are taken up, not diminished nor destroyed, but celebrated and renewed, purified if need be, and fulfilled (as the Second Vatican Council teaches) in the life of the Spirit" (IMC 15).

Two workshop papers (V and VII) of the Manila Mission Congress spoke eloquently of the local Church. The participants of Workshop VII noted: "We recognize that the local church is the center and source of evangelization" (1). "Just as it is the responsibility of the Christian to work for the growth and development of the local church, in the same way he must become aware of his responsibility toward churches in other parts of the world" (9). This means: "Each local church is co-responsible with its sister churches everywhere, Rome being the foundation and center, for the building up of the kingdom of God throughout the world" (9).

The same document of Workshop VII affirms that "Missionaries from sister churches are not only living signs of the universality of the Church and the existence of co-responsibility, but because of their different cultural and Christian background, they enrich and fruitfully challenge the local church. The local church should welcome, accept and help integrate them into its life" (10).

FABC III. The Third FABC Plenary Assembly in 1982 chose "The Church—A Community of Faith in Asia" as its central theme. Again, one finds enlightening words on the local Church. The final FABC III statement noted: "We have seen … how the local church must be a community of graced communion rooted in the life of the Trinity, a community of prayer and contemplation, and of sacramental celebration and life centered around the Eucharist. It must be defined by its life of faithful discipleship in the Gospel, patterned on the Paschal Mystery of Jesus, 'a community for others.' We have realized that genuine participation and co-responsibility must be essential elements of its existence, and theological reflection and discernment integral components of its life. It is a community which strives to remain in unfeigned unity with its pastors, within the bonds of local and universal communion in the one Church" (FABC III, 15).

Theses on the Local Church. The centrality of the local Church in the theological-missiological thought in the Asian area is highlighted by the FABC commitment to study the question in depth. The FABC has promoted indigenous Asian theological reflection since its early years; the formal establishment of the Theological Advisory Commission (TAC) of the FABC came in the 1980s. A five-year period of extensive study and consultation culminated in a comprehensive document entitled "Theses on the Local Church: A Theological Reflection in the Asian Context" (TLC). This is one of the longest documents ever produced by the TAC (well over 50 closely printed pages); it was released in January 1991. In the opinion of this author, worldwide it is probably the best and most comprehensive document to date on *local Church*.

The FABC-TAC document on the local Church contains several sections. After a lengthy contextualized introduction and clarification of terms, the fifteen theses are presented in two thematic sections: "Biblical Foundations" (Theses 1-4) and "The Birth, Life and Mission of the Local Church" (Theses 5-15). Next, a concluding section follows; finally, a wide variety of practical "Pastoral Corollaries and Recommendations" are presented. Some salient quotes serve to capture the spirit of this insightful piece of Asian theological reflection.

"Already, as we have noted, the First Plenary Assembly of the FABC spoke of building up of the local Church as the present focus of the Church's mission in Asia. That discernment remains valid today [1991].... More and more the local Churches in Asia must see themselves as responsible agents for the self-realization of the Church" (TLC: C, 3-4).

"We see the emergence of the world of the Third Millennium already upon us.... Whether the Gospel shall be present in this new age with its unpredictable turnings and its manifold diversity will depend greatly on whether local Churches fulfill their vocation in the historic moment which is now upon them. We grasp something of the significance of local Church and inculturation in this context; those who cannot understand this fail to resonate with the signs of our time, and the heartbeat of our peoples" (TLC: C, 5).

"We must surely be grateful that we experience today the 'rush of the Spirit' in our Churches. For it is a privileged moment for local theological reflection and discernment, for the gathering and spending of energies, for the upbuilding of authentic local Churches in our part of the world.... We can only pray that we may listen and be obedient to the Spirit, that we may be guided by his creative power and be filled by the commitment and courage which are his gifts" (TLC: C, 6-7).

FABC IV. The Fourth FABC Plenary Assembly in 1986 focused on the theme: "The Vocation and Mission of the Laity in the Church and in the World of Asia." Set in the context of "the task of the Church in the world of Asia" (FABC IV, 2.2), the assembly focused heavily on various concrete areas where the laity makes its contribution to serving the local Church and the peoples of Asia.

An impressive panorama of the various involvements of the laity was explored: politics, youth, women, family, education, mass media, work, business, health services, community, liberation, lay apostolates, clergy-laity relationships, formation, spirituality, and kingdom theology. Treatment of each of these specific topics is beyond the scope of this presentation; one need only assert that clearly the theology of local Church underpins these many areas of engagement.

FABC V. Most major documents of the FABC refer explicitly to the role of the local Church in mission and evangelization. The Fifth Plenary FABC Assembly in 1990, with the theme "Journeying Together toward the Third Millennium," added new clarity and focus by asserting that it is the local Church which is "the acting subject of mission."

"The renewal of our sense of mission will mean ... that the acting subject of mission is the *local church* living and acting in communion with the universal Church. It is the local churches and communities which can discern and work out (in dialogue with each other and with other persons of goodwill) the way the Gospel is best proclaimed, the Church set up, the values of God's Kingdom realized in their own place and time. In fact, it is by responding to and serving the needs of the peoples of Asia that the different Christian communities become truly local churches" (FABC V, 3.3.1).

"This local church, which is the acting subject of mission, is the people of God in a given milieu, the whole Christian community—laity, Religious and clergy. It is the whole diocese, the parish, the Basic Ecclesial Community and other groups. Their time has come for Asia" (FABC V, 3.3.2).

FABC VI. The Sixth FABC Plenary Assembly in 1995 in conjunction with the visit of Pope John Paul II for the World Youth Day summarized key themes of the 25-year history of FABC. The final statement entitled "Christian Discipleship in Asia Today: Service to Life" noted that: "The overall thrust of activities in recent years has been to motivate the Churches of Asia towards 'a new way of being Church,' a Church that is committed to becoming 'a community of communities' and a credible sign of salvation and liberation" (FABC VI, 3). "It is the Spirit of Jesus that creates the [Church as a] disciple-community" (FABC VI, 14).

Many are the challenges of being an authentic local Church in Asia. Asian Catholics admit: "We may hesitate because we are a minority group. Indeed we are a little flock in Asia. But it is from this position of weakness that God's gift of divine life in Jesus Crucified, the power and wisdom of God, is most significant" (FABC VI, 14.3). Most local Churches in Asia continually discover and live their identities as minorities within their national societies.

Asian Synod Echoes FABC Themes. A short excursus provides interesting insights into key FABC themes about local Church that resounded in the Special Assembly for Asia of the Synod of Bishops ("Asian Synod") held in Rome from April 19-May 14, 1998. As Cardinal Stephen Kim Sou-hwan of Korea greeted the Holy Father and the Synod participants in his opening address on April 20, he described the realities of Asia which "is made up not of various nations but, one may say, many worlds."

Kim noted the endeavors and accomplishments of the FABC "for the past 27 years"; in building up a truly local Church in Asia "continual and quite serious efforts have been made to listen to, learn from, and reflect and act upon today's lived Asian realities in faith and prayer. And, we have felt called to an ever renewed self-understanding of the Church and her mission, not so much from abstract thought, but in the face of given pastoral situations and their exigencies" (OR-EE: April 29, 1998: 5).

Bishop Josef Suwatan, MSC, of Indonesia asserted that the "peoples of Asia need the witness of 'being Church'." He pointed out how "the Fifth Plenary Assembly of FABC in 1990 in Bandung speaks about 'a new way of being Church' in Asia, as a 'communion of communities'." He reiterated: "Note well, it speaks about 'being' Church!" (OR-EE: April 29, 1998: 15). Again, Archbishop Petrus Turang of Indonesia echoed the same theme and focused on the growth of the local Churches: "The Churches of Asia need to take advantage of the vision of a new way of being Church" (OR-EE: May 20, 1998: 8). This new approach will also achieve, according to Bishop John Cummins, "the desired communion among local Churches"; this means accepting "the Federation of Asian Bishops' Conferences as a vehicle to do this" (OR-EE: May 20, 1998: 13).

The missionary dimension of the local Churches of Asia emerged strongly in the Synod. Father Edward Malone, FABC Assistant Secretary General, emphasized several crucial points: "Asian Christians and local Churches have a deep sense of gratitude for the gift of faith.... With the renewal of ecclesiology a wide variety of mission initiatives must necessarily emerge from within each local Church...." Concretely, specific actions must help promote "the emergence of missionary local Churches"; thus, "pastoral care is not to derail the local Church mission effort" and "the actual foundation of Asian-born missionary societies is to be fostered in each local Church" (OR-EE: May 13, 1998: 14).

Several Synod interventions focused on the challenges of this FABC-inspired "new way of being Church." Bishop Pakiam of Malaysia captured the essence of this commitment to "be witnesses of the Gospel as a community of the local Church in a multiracial, multicultural, multilinguistic country"; note that this description reflects the reality of most Asian countries. Bishop Pakiam recommended following FABC directions so that local Churches become "a communion of communities, a participatory Church, a dialoguing and prophetic Church" (OR-EE: June 17, 1998: 8).

In the final session of the Synod on May 13, Cardinal Darmaatmadja of Indonesia again referred to the task of "being Church in Asia." For him all local Churches must struggle to be "a Church with an Asian 'face' [and an] Asian appearance"; they must avoid appearing "foreign to Asia's traditions and cultures" (OR-EE: June 17, 1998: 10-11). In a word, they must emerge as truly *local Churches*!

FABC Themes in Ecclesia in Asia. The Apostolic Exhortation *Ecclesia in Asia* promulgated by Pope John

Paul II in New Delhi, India on November 6, 1999 echoed the ecclesiology of the Asian Synod Fathers of the FABC region. Although the document develops the "ecclesiology of communion" extensively, significant insights on the local Churches of Asia are found within the papal exhortation.

Ecclesia in Asia notes that "the Synod Fathers were well aware of the pressing need of the local Churches in Asia to present the mystery of Christ according to their cultural patterns and ways of thinking" (20). It is necessary that "each local Church should become what the Synod Fathers called a 'participatory Church,' a Church, that is, in which all live their proper vocation and perform their proper role" (25). The pope's exhortation praises the Federation of Asian Bishops' Conferences by name, because it has "helped to foster union among the local Churches" and has "provided venues for cooperation in resolving pastoral problems" (26).

In *Ecclesia in Asia* Pope John Paul II identifies important responsibilities of the local Churches in Asia: "where possible the local Churches in Asia should promote human rights activities on behalf of women" (34); "local Churches, for their part, need to foster awareness of the ideal of the religious and consecrated life, and promote such vocations" (44); mission is the task of each local Church, and the pope recommends "the establishment within each local Church of Asia, where such do not exist, of missionary societies of apostolic life, characterized by their special commitment to the mission *ad gentes, ad exteros* and *ad vitam*" (44).

John Paul II continues: "the local Churches in Asia, in communion with the Successor of Peter, need to foster greater communion of mind and heart through close cooperation among themselves" (24); Church unity also respects "the legitimate diversity of the local Churches and the variety of cultures and peoples with which they are in contact" (25).

FABC VII. The Seventh FABC Plenary Assembly, the first major Church gathering of the Jubilee Year 2000, was held from January 3-12, 2000. The assembly of 193 participants (cardinals, bishops, clergy, religious, and laity) explored the theme: "A Renewed Church in Asia: A Mission of Love and Service." Once again, the integrating theology of local Church came to the fore in the final statement.

The participants asserted: "from the depths of Asia's hopes and anxieties, we hear the call of the Spirit to the local churches in Asia. It is a call to renewal, to a renewed mission of love and service. It is a call to the local churches to be faithful to Asian cultural, spiritual and social values and thus to be truly inculturated local churches" (FABC VII: Introduction).

The assembly reflected: "The thirty-year history of the FABC has been a concerted series of movements toward a renewed Church." Of the eight movements noted, one pivotal initiative has been the "movement toward a 'truly local Church,' toward a Church 'incarnate in a people, a Church indigenous and inculturated'." The assembly statement boldly affirmed: "This is the vision of a renewed Church that the FABC has developed over the past thirty years. It is still valid today" (FABC VII: I-A).

FABC VIII. For the first time in its history, the FABC held its plenary assembly in Korea in Korea. The theme of the 2004 gathering was: "The Asian Family towards a Culture of Integral Life." The assembled bishops expressed their hope that the assembly would provide a "deeper reflection on the Asian family in view of relevant and effective pastoral care" (FABC VIII: 5).

Relating the family to the Church, the bishops asserted: "The family is the basic cell of society and the fundamental ecclesial community, the Church that is the home. In Asia today there is a growing realization that the family has to be the focus of integral evangelization and the essential building block of the BEC/BHC [Basic Ecclesial Community / Basic Human Community] and *even of the local Church as a whole* [emphasis supplied]. In other words, the Church begins in the home" (FABC VIII: 46).

Later, in the same final document of the plenary assembly,

it is noted: "May it not even be said that the focal point of evangelization should be the family as object and subject, to which all parish pastoral programs are geared? The BEC would then be a community of families, and the parish truly a community of communities.... It is in these communities, at the level of the family, where the 'globalization of charity and solidarily' begins" (FABC VIII: 100).

FABC IX. "Living the Eucharist in Asia" was the central theme of the Ninth FABC Plenary Assembly held in Manila, Philippines in 2009 (originally scheduled for Bangalore, India). The assembly sought to integrate the insights of two recent international synods on the Eucharist (2005) and on the Word of God (2008), examining the synodal reflections in reference to the challenges of "a new way of being Church" in the Asian context. The discussions had a decidedly "pastoral" focus; the emphasis centered, not on the "believing" dimension (doctrinal faith) or the "celebrating" aspects (liturgical practice) of the Eucharist, but on the "living" ramifications (concrete praxis) of Eucharist within the realities of daily life in Asia.

As the Eighth FABC Plenary Assembly focused primarily on the family, this gathering took the Eucharist as its central focus. Thus, in both cases little is specifically said about the "local" Church. Yet, in this assembly one finds inspiring references to the missionary identity of the "entire" Church. "Every Eucharistic celebration renews the Church in its missionary calling. By its very nature as the bearer of the Good News of Jesus Christ, the Church is missionary. Only by being true to its mission can it remain true to its identity" (FABC IX: E-4). "In Asia, the missionary witness of the Church is a way of living the Eucharist.... The dynamism of the Eucharist becomes the rhythm of life of the followers of Christ. The Eucharist forms the Church.... [and] is the life of the Church" (FABC IX: F).

FABC X. Gathering for the first time in its history in Vietnam in 2012, the FABC took up the theme: "FABC at Forty Years— Responding to the Challenges of Asia: New Evangelization." The gathering noted how the previous nine plenary assemblies had "provided the principal themes of renewal for the Local Churches in Asia" and that they "affirmed that the acting subject of mission is *the local church*, incarnated and rooted firmly in the culture of its people, taking up their strengths as well as their weaknesses in the light of the healing and redeeming grace of Christ" (FABC X: 5).

The assembled bishops asserted that "the Church has to be a humble servant. She is *a community-in-mission, a disciple-community* in the footsteps of the Lord Jesus who came to serve and not to be served. Christian discipleship in Asia, the Asian Bishops affirm, has to be a *service to life*" (FABC X: 7). "We thank the Lord for a challenging *vision of Church in Asia*. This vision of Church has been the over-all objective of the pastoral reflection, discernment, prayer, and pastoral action of the FABC through the years" (FABC X: 11). "The FABC process has been truly a dialogue among local churches.... The communion of local churches is marvelously enriched.... The Lord has, indeed, blessed FABC through and in each of its members for the mission of evangelization that he has entrusted to the Church in Asia" (FABC X: 15). Undoubtedly, the FABC vision of a "new way of being Church" has taken flesh in Asia over the past four decades (1972-2012)!

Conclusion. The experience of the pilgrim local Churches in Asia since Vatican II has been an exciting and inspiring faith-journey. It has been an experience in *ecclesiogenesis*, the birthing and development of local Churches. It has verified the ancient adage that the Church is always *in via*, on the road, in process—as she awaits her Lord and Savior, Jesus Christ. The road has not been a well-trodden path; Asian Churches are making the pilgrim way in the very process of walking it—under the guidance of the befriending Spirit. Asian Christians "see themselves as responsible agents for the self-realization of the Church" (TLC: C-4). They experientially know that they are "the acting subject of mission" (FABC V, 3.3.1). They rejoice in their "new way of being Church" (FABC VI, 3). The dream of vibrant local Churches within an authentic catholicity continues to grow and take on flesh. Christians frequently meditate on the wondrous mystery that in the power of the Spirit the Church is for believers *donum Dei atque officium nostri*, at one and the same time, both God's gift and our task!

"PASTORAL SPIRAL" METHODOLOGY

How do the local Churches of Asia envision implementing their insights on being Church and fulfilling their mission? How will the Church in Asia be a "communion of communities," "a participatory Church," and an "inculturated local Church" that "witnesses to the Risen Lord"? In response to these perennial questions, the FABC has evolved a unique approach of pastoral engagement. This four-stage "Asian" methodology has been termed: the "Pastoral Spiral" (cf. BISA VII, 8-13).

The process begins with *exposure-immersion*; it may also be called "entering into a dialogue-of-life." Exposure-Immersion follows the basic principle of the Incarnation; local Christians seek to share the daily lives of their neighbors and communities. They seek to understand and appreciate— through direct experience and interaction—the life situation shared by Muslims, Buddhists, Hindus, and Christians. In a word, all are invited to practice "good neighbor-ology."

The second stage of *social analysis* follows. Communities try to evaluate the social, economic, political, cultural, and religious systems in society. They observe and analyze events and trends, discerning the impact of rapid social change on human lives. They evaluate the signs of the times, the voices of the contemporary age, the events of history, as well as the needs and aspirations of people and communities. It is an interfaith effort to comprehend the realities that shape their lives.

Asians have seen the necessity of integrating social analysis (stage two) with the *contemplative dimension* (stage three) of evangelization and human development; this third stage of faith reflection emerges from Asia's religio-cultural heritage.

Through this contemplation people discover God's presence and activity within social realities, discerning not only negative and enslaving social aspects, but also the positive, prophetic aspects of life that can inspire genuine God-awareness and spirituality. This stage in the total process has proven very beneficial; for example, it enables the poor to make their unique contribution to the Church's mission; it brings prayer and spirituality into the endeavor.

The third stage of ongoing spiritual-theological reflection issues into the fourth stage called *pastoral planning*, which seeks to translate the previous three stages into actual, realizable mission plans of action. Indeed, concrete programs of evangelization are ultimately necessary, but they are better conceived through this Asian process that actively discerns what the Lord of history is challenging the Church to be and to do.

One should note that this process is a *spiral*—it must be repeated frequently; hopefully, at each turn or cycle it moves upward and forward. The local Churches in Asia have committed themselves to this demanding approach to mission and evangelization.

A final, brief "footnote" may be added to link the FABC pastoral spiral with the "see, judge, act" methodology, traditionally associated with programs of Catholic Action. This approach to social transformation encourages Christians to "see" (observe concrete social realities), "judge" (analyze and evaluate these realities), and "act" (make decisions and take concrete steps to transform the reality). FABC V has enunciated a similar approach, expressed with the "3-D" terminology; Asian Churches must "dialogue" with life's realities, then prayerfully "discern" the situation in faith, and lastly, engage in appropriate Christ-like "deeds" to transform the situation (cf. FABC V, 4.1-4.6). There are, ultimately, many parallels in these inductive pastoral approaches (whatever name one may give to them); the crucial factor is that the Christian community, motivated by faith and the Gospel values of the Kingdom, remains actively engaged in the transformation of the world.

"ASIAN-BORN" MISSION INITIATIVES

The foregoing panorama of significant FABC contributions to forming inculturated local Churches with a commitment to evangelization can be augmented by a description of the "Asian-born" missionary societies. Significantly, all these societies have been founded in the Vatican II era. They are: Mission Society of the Philippines: MSP (1965); Mission Society of Saint Thomas the Apostle [India]: MST (1968); Catholic Foreign Mission Society of Korea: KMS (1975); Thailand Mission Society: TMS (1990); and, Lorenzo Ruiz Mission Society [Philippines]: LRMS (1997). Currently, Vietnam and Myanmar are in the process of establishing their own missionary groups; Indonesia is also exploring some concrete options to become further engaged in *ad gentes* mission.

In addition, to their uniqueness as "Asian-born" mission societies of the Vatican II era, these five missionary communities reflect a specific charism: Mission Society of Apostolic Life. Three characteristics describe their unique identity and mission contribution: *Ad Gentes*, *Ad Exteros*, and *Ad Vitam*. Such societies direct their efforts of evangelization *ad gentes* (to those who have not yet heard the liberating and salvific Good News of Jesus Christ), *ad exteros* (to peoples outside their own country, cultural milieu, and language group), and *ad vitam* (through a life-long commitment to this unique form of missionary witness). The Asian Synod (Proposition 28) and *Ecclesia in Asia* (44) specifically recommended "the establishment within each local Church of Asia, where such do not exist, of missionary societies of apostolic life."

FABC perspectives and insights have certainly been integrated into the mission approaches of these "Asian-born" missionary groups. In addition, FABC's Office of Evangelization (OE) has been promoting missionary cooperation among the five Asian-born Missionary Societies of Apostolic Life (AMSAL). This AMSAL group, now a semi-autonomous organization, began with a FABC-sponsored gathering in Thailand (1997).

Although modest in its organization, AMSAL continues to promote renewal and cooperation through its Asian assemblies held on odd-numbered years; AMSAL members join the world-wide gatherings of **M**issionary **S**ocieties of **A**postolic **L**ife (MISAL) held on the even-numbered years. AMSAL hosted the MISAL in Bangkok in January of 2004, focusing on the topic of interreligious dialogue and contemporary mission. The initial history, vision, and activities of AMSAL are documented in the book *Asia-Church in Mission* (1999) and in *FABC Papers 88.*

More specifically, how has the mission vision of the *ad gentes* missionary institutes been implemented in Asia? To answer this question concretely, a very succinct synopsis of each Asian-born missionary society will be presented. As noted earlier, the commonality of all these "Vatican II" mission institutes lies in their unique and specific missionary charism: *ad gentes, ad exteros,* and *ad vitam.* All are focused on "apostolic" life; they do *not* pronounce "religious" vows, though they bind themselves permanently *(ad vitam)* for specifically *ad gentes* and *ad exteros* mission. One must note that there are some other "Asia-born" religious institutes that focus on mission, but they are religious congregations with vows (thus, not technically mission societies of apostolic life).

Missionary Society of the Philippines. On the fourth centenary of the evangelization of the Philippine Islands (1565-1965) the Catholic Hierarchy declared that "to express in the concrete our gratitude to God for the gift of our Faith we will organize the Foreign Mission Society of the Philippines." The official or statutory name of the society is: Mission Society of the Philippines (MSP), often popularly referred to as "Fil-Mission." It is a Filipino clerical mission society of apostolic life of pontifical right.

The MSP defines its charism in these words: "In love and gratitude to the Father, ours is a joyful missionary spirit flowing from deep union with Christ through Mary and in the power of the Holy Spirit, willing to spend and be spent in sharing His Gospel to all." The Catholic bishops of the Philippines have designated one Sunday each year as "Fil-Mission Sunday" to help support MSP as a commitment of the entire local Church.

Membership in the MSP is open to natural-born Filipinos; the Society also welcomes Filipino diocesan priests as associate members to serve in foreign mission. The MSP considers its mission apostolate in *de jure* and *de facto* mission territories as its foremost duty and privilege. Asia has always been the highest priority in the choice of mission apostolates.

In the first years of the new millennium (2000-2004) the MSP undertook several new mission initiatives: (a) care for the numerous Filipino migrants so as to enable them to become active partners in the work of evangelization; (b) establishment of a mission center in Thailand focused on the aged and sick, especially those affected with AIDS; (c) opening of additional "frontier" mission stations in Papua New Guinea; and, (d) organization of mission animation programs for local lay faithful focused on mission ad gentes.

Missionary Society of Saint Thomas the Apostle. The Missionary Society of Saint Thomas the Apostle (MST) in India is an indigenous missionary institute of the Syro-Malabar Church. In 1960, Mar Sebastian Vayalil sought the permission of the Holy See to found a mission society. Rome asked Bishop Vayalil to submit a draft constitution of the proposed society in 1963; he accomplished this in 1964. The nascent society began as a Pius Union of Diocesan Clergy in 1965. Additional steps were taken, and the MST was founded at Deepti Nagar, Melampara, Bharananganam on February 22, 1968. The founding members of MST were 18 diocesan priests who made their Promise of Incorporation to MST on July 16, 1968. On July 3, 1997 the MST was raised to a "Society of Apostolic Life of Major Archiepiscopal Right"; equivalently, this corresponds to "Pontifical Right" in the Roman Church. The scope of the Society is "mission *ad gentes*" in the less Christian regions of India and beyond, "remaining faithful to the heritage and identity of the Syro-Malabar Church."

The growth of MST in the first decades of existence has been phenomenal. In 1993 when the MST celebrated its silver jubilee, the Syro-Malabar bishops through a joint pastoral letter again owned the Society and exhorted the faithful to support its missionary activities.

New mission activities undertaken in the early years of the third millennium are focused on prison ministry (services, rehabilitation and reintegration of released prisoners), care of HIV/AIDS patients, mission animation in the Church of origin, and the establishment of a missiological research center. MST superiors noted four important mission challenges: Hindu fundamentalism in India, consumerist society's negative influence on missioners themselves, slackening spirituality, and less enthusiasm of personnel to take up challenging missions.

The evaluation of the positive results achieved in mission noted the following areas of growth: prison ministry, women empowerment programs, rehabilitation programs for the physically and mentally challenged, as well as programs for street children. The constant growth of MST is a significant factor, providing a sense of optimism as well as allowing for the implementing of new mission endeavors.

Catholic Foreign Mission Society of Korea. In late 1974 a Korean preparation committee was established to explore the possible formation of a mission society. By a decision of the Korean Bishops' Conference, the Korean Foreign Mission Society was founded on February 26, 1975. A formation house was opened in 1976, and the first priest for the society was ordained in 1981. In the same year the first missionary was sent to Papua New Guinea.

The KMS (Korean Mission Society) seeks to proclaim the Gospel and imitate Jesus Christ, the model for all missionaries. "We also model ourselves on the evangelical spirit of the 103 Korean martyrs who witnessed to Jesus even unto their death." They also "make a preferential option for the poor and are in solidarity with their spiritual and material sufferings." In the new millennium, the KMS took some new mission initiatives. It began mission in Cambodia and Russia in 2001; it established a small mission research center in 2004; it opened a mission presence in Mozambique in 2005.

In response to a Mission Societies Questionnaire, the KMS noted three specific challenges it currently faces: (a) the recruitment of vocations in Korea, where nationally there is a low birth-rate at present; (b) the ongoing effort to stabilize KMS mission funds; and, (c) the challenge to instill a deeper mission consciousness among the Catholics of South Korea. The hope is that the newly established mission research center will help to address these difficulties.

Thailand Missionary Society. In March 1987, the Superior of the Paris Foreign Mission Society in Thailand addressed a letter to the Bishops' Conference suggesting the formation of a missionary group of Thai priests. They were to work with the Hill Tribe peoples in northern Thailand. The idea was well received by the bishops; contacts were made with diocesan seminarians, religious congregations, and lay people. The responsibility for the project came to rest upon Bishop Banchong Aribang from Nakorn Sawan.

In 1989 four seminarians volunteered to become members of the Society. In June 1990 and in January 1991 the first two priests were ordained for the Thailand Missionary Society (TMS); this is considered the real beginning of TMS (popularly called the "Thai Missionary Society"). This society of secular priests aims to do "apostolic work among those who do not know Jesus Christ in Thailand and out of Thailand." Currently, they serve in Northern Thailand among the Hill Tribe peoples as well as in Cambodia. Planning has been undertaken to assist the Church in Laos, knowing full well that for the time being, it is impossible to send anyone inside Laos.

As a Society of Apostolic Life, TMS is responsible to the Bishops' Conference of Thailand; the bishops appoint the superior of the society. Full members are secular, diocesan priests who join the society with the approval of their bishop; they keep a special relationship with their home diocese, even though they are incardinated into the TMS. There is a fine relationship between the TMS and the Bishops' Conference of Thailand; good financial support comes from the Bishops, but additional personnel from them would be appreciated. Given the small number of members, there is no current plan to expand beyond the present mission commitments.

Lorenzo Ruiz Mission Society. In 1949 during civil disturbances in China, the Saint Joseph Regional Seminary which was under Jesuit administration was transferred to Manila. In the ensuing years about 60 Chinese seminarians were ordained in the Philippines; they went on to found 14 Filipino-Chinese parishes and 18 Filipino-Chinese schools.

To facilitate the continuation of these apostolates and to recruit and train younger clergy, Jaime Cardinal Sin of Manila established the Lorenzo Mission Institute (a Filipino-Chinese seminary) in 1987. Pope John Paul II has also requested Cardinal Sin to help prepare missionaries for China. During the Pope's January 1995 sojourn in Manila, he visited this seminary, instructing the Cardinal to "maintain and preserve the said seminary at all cost."

In this context the Lorenzo Ruiz Mission Society (LRMS) has been formed; it received its decree of approval from Cardinal Sin on January 14, 1997. It is a Clerical Society of Apostolic Life of diocesan right with its ecclesiastical seat in the Archdiocese of Manila. The LRMS is "intrinsically and eminently missionary in spirit and finality." The LRMS draws its inspiration from Saint Lorenzo, the first Filipino saint who was of mixed Filipino and Chinese descent; he was martyred in Japan where he went as a lay catechist with Spanish Dominican friars in the 1600s.

One important initiative that the LRMS has taken is the formation of future priests from the People's Republic of China. Some priests have returned to China; others still remain outside

China for further studies and experience. One of these alumni priests was ordained bishop on January 6, 2004 in China under very difficult circumstances. As an integral part of its mission vision, the LRMS takes concrete steps to keep the local Church-of-origin focused on its *ad gentes* missionary obligations.

As a final note to this section, one must observe that a complete panorama of Asian mission initiatives would also have to include the numerous Asians that are serving in ad gentes mission through international societies of religious women and men. Various lay movements also send personnel for evangelization in many Asian nations; for example, lay mission movements have been established in Japan, Philippines, and Hong Kong. The vast majority of these missionaries serve in other Asian countries. Inspired by the FABC vision as well as local theologies, spiritualities, and pastoral visions, there are many Asians committed to evangelizing their Asian neighbors.

CONCLUDING REFLECTON

This presentation has highlighted some significant Asian developments in mission vision, theology, and pastoral practice since the Second Vatican Council; it has described the "Good News from Asia" about mission. Special emphasis was given to some of the pivotal contributions made by the FABC. Other areas of mission fostered by the FABC could have been chosen (e.g. laity, social communications, liberation and development, etc.); however, those presented here provide a foundational orientation to the remarkable contribution by the FABC for the renewal of the Church in Asia. This piece has also shown how Asia's local Churches have tried to follow the Gospel injunction: "What you have received as a gift, give as a gift" (Mt 10:8).

Pope John Paul II has frequently referred to the third millennium as the Asian Millennium in mission (e.g. EA 1-2); this challenge has been received with optimism and commitment by the local Churches in Asia. They have rededicated themselves to proclaiming Christ, his Gospel, his love, his compassion, to billions of Asians who have not yet come to know Jesus. For

Asia's local Churches, her mission societies, her laity, religious, and clergy, the Church's mission is pivotal to her very life and future. To be and become the Church is a solid commitment. Authentic Christian living and joyous evangelizing always go hand-in-hand—in Asia and throughout the entire missionary Church. For all mature Christians, *to live is to evangelize!*

ABBREVIATIONS

ACMC	- Asian Colloquium on Ministries in the Church (Hong Kong: 1977)
AG	- *Ad Gentes* (December 7, 1965)
AMSAL	- Asian-born Missionary Societies of Apostolic Life
BISA	- FABC Bishops' Institutes for Social Action
EA	- *Ecclesia in Asia* (November 6, 1999)
EN	- *Evangelii Nuntiandi* (December 8, 1975)
FABC	- Federation of Asian Bishops' Conferences
FABC I	- First FABC Plenary Assembly (Taiwan: 1974)
FABC II	- Second FABC Plenary Assembly (India: 1978)
FABC III	- Third FABC Plenary Assembly (Thailand: 1982)
FABC IV	- Fourth FABC Plenary Assembly (Japan: 1986)
FABC V	- Fifth FABC Plenary Assembly (Indonesia: 1990)
FABC VI	- Sixth FABC Plenary Assembly (Philippines: 1995)
FABC VII	- Seventh FABC Plenary Assembly (Thailand: 2000)
FABC VIII	- Eighth FABC Plenary Assembly (Korea: 2004)
FABC IX	- Ninth FABC Plenary Assembly (Philippines: 2009)
FABC X	- Tenth FABC Plenary Assembly (Vietnam: 2012)
FABC:OE	- FABC: Office of Evangelization
IMC	- International Mission Congress (Philippines: 1979)
KMS	- Korean Mission Society
LRMS	- Lorenzo Ruiz Mission Society
MISAL	- Missionary Societies of Apostolic Life
MSP	- Missionary Society of the Philippines
MST	- Missionary Society of Saint Thomas the Apostle
OR-EE	- *L'Osservatore Romano* (English Edition)
RM	- *Redemptoris Missio* (December 7, 1990)
TAC	- Theological Advisory Commission of the FABC
TLC	- *Theses on the Local Church* (FABC)
TMS	- Thailand Missionary Society

ASIA'S LOCAL CHURCHES AND MISSION
A Selected Bibliography

Agustinus, B. *A Study on the Evangelizing Mission of the Church in Contemporary Asia in the Light of the Documents of the Federation of Asian Bishops' Conferences, 1970-1995.* Doctoral Thesis in Theology, Rome: Pontifical Urban University, 1997.

Arévalo, C. **(A)** "The Church as a Community of Faith," *FABC Papers 29.* Hong Kong: FABC Secretariat, 1982; **(B)** "The Church in Asia and Mission in the 1990s," *FABC Papers 57b.* Hong Kong: FABC Secretariat, 1990; **(C)** "Mission in the 1990s," *International Bulletin of Missionary Research* 14:2 (April, 1990): 50-53; **(D)** "Self-Portrait: A Life in the Service of the Church in the Philippines and of Asia," In *Jahrbuch für Kontextuelle Theologien 1995.* **G. Evers** (Ed.)., 7-52. Aachen, Germany: Missionswissen-schaftliches Institut Missio e.V., 1995; similar presentation in: *Landas* 25 (2011): 307-351.

Colombo, D. *Documenti della Chiesa in Asia: Federazione delle Conferenze Episcopali Asiatiche: 1970-1995.* Bologna: Editrice Missionaria Italiana, 1997.

Darmaatmadja, J. "A Church with a Truly Asian Face," *Origins* 28:2 (May 28, 1998): 24-28.

Dulles, A. and **P. Granfield.** (Eds.). "The Particular or Local Church" 132-135 and "Asian Ecclesiology" 173-174. In *The Theology of the Church: A Bibliography.* New York: Paulist Press, 1999.

Eilers, F. (Ed.). **(A)** *For All the Peoples of Asia II: Federation of Asian Bishops' Conferences Documents from 1992 to 1996.* Quezon City, Philippines: Claretian Publications, 1997; **(B)** *For All the Peoples of Asia III: Federation of Asian Bishops' Conferences Documents from 1997 to 2001.* Quezon City, Philippines: Claretian Publications, 2002; **(C)** *For All the Peoples of Asia IV: Federation of Asian Bishops' Conferences*

Documents from 2002 to 2006. Quezon City, Philippines: Claretian Publications, 2007.

Emmanuel, S. (A) "Local Churches and the World Church," *East Asian Pastoral Review* 27:1 (1990): 59-75; **(B)** "Asian Churches for a New Evangelization: Chances and Challenges," *East Asian Pastoral Review* 36:3 (1999): 252-275.

Evers, G. (Ed.). *Bibliography on Local Church in Asia* [*Theology in Context Supplements 3*]. Aachen, Germany: Institute of Missiology, 1989.

FABC:TAC (Federation of Asian Bishops' Conferences: Theological Advisory Commission). "Theses on the Local Church: A Theological Reflection in the Asian Context," In *Being Church in Asia*, **J. Gnanapiragasam** and **F. Wilfred** (Eds.)., 33-89. Quezon City, Philippines: Claretian Publications, 1994; [see: *FABC Papers 60*: 1-58].

Fitzpatrick, M. *Bishop Francisco F. Claver, SJ on the Local Church (1972-1990).* Manila: De La Salle University Press, Inc., 1995 [Extensive Bibliography].

Fox, T. *Pentecost in Asia: A New Way of Being Church.* Maryknoll, NY: Orbis Books, 2002.

Hai, P. (A) "The Laity in Historical Context," *East Asian Pastoral Review* 46 (2009): 334-356; **(B)** "Features of the FABC's Theology of the Laity," *East Asian Pastoral Review* 47 (2010): 7-37; **(C)** "Evaluation of the FABC's Theology of the Laity," *East Asian Pastoral Review* 47 (2010): 234-262; **(D)** "Reflections on the Future of the FABC's Theology of the Laity," *East Asian Pastoral Review* 49 (2012): 107-132.

Handoko, P. *Lay Ministries in the Mission and Ministry of the Church in Asia: A Critical Study of the Documents of the FABC, 1970-1991.* Doctoral Thesis in Theology, Rome: Pontifical Gregorian University, 1993.

Hardawiryana, R. "The Missionary Dimensions of the Local Church: Asia and Indonesia," In *Mission in Dialogue*. **M. Motte** and **J. Lang** (Eds.)., 34-72. Maryknoll, NY: Orbis Books, 1982.

Hennesey, J. "The Ecclesiology of the Local Church: A Historian's Look," *Thought* 66:263 (1991): 368-375.

Heyndrickx, J. "The Emergence of a Local Catholic Church in China?" *Tripod* 37 (1987): 51-75.

Kavunkal, J. "Local Church in the FABC Statements," *Jeevadhara* 27:160 (1997): 260-271.

Keeler, W. "Bishops' Conferences: Servants of Communion between the Local and Universal Church," *Origins* 31:18 (October 11, 2001): 304-306.

Komonchak, J. **(A)** "The Church Universal as the Communion of Local Churches," In *Where Does the Church Stand?* **G. Alberigo** and **G. Gutierrez** (Eds.)., 30-35. New York: The Seabury Press, 1981; **(B)** "Towards a Theology of the Local Church," *FABC Papers 42*. Hong Kong: FABC Secretariat, 1986; **(C)** "The Local Realization of the Church," In *The Reception of Vatican II*. **G. Alberigo** *et al*. (Eds.)., 77-90. Washington, DC: The Catholic University of America Press, 1987; **(D)** "The Church: God's Gift and Our Task," *Origins* 16:42 (April 2, 1987): 735-741; **(E)** "The Local Church," *Chicago Studies* 28:3 (November, 1989): 320-335; **(F)** "Many Models, One Church," *Church* 9:1 (Spring, 1993): 12-15.

Kroeger, J. **(A)** *Asia-Church in Mission*. Quezon City, Philippines: Claretian Publications, 1999; **(B)** "Rejoice, O Asia-Church!" *East Asian Pastoral Review* 37:3 (2000): 278-285; **(C)** "A Continuing Pentecost: Appreciating '*Ecclesia in Asia*'," *Review for Religious* 60:1 (January-February, 2001): 20-29; **(D)** "FABC Papers Comprehensive Index (1976-2001)," *FABC Papers 100*. Hong Kong: FABC Secretariat, 2001: 1-58; an expanded version is found in *For All the Peoples of Asia IV*. Quezon City,

Philippines: Claretian Publications, 2007: Appendix II; **(E)** Edited with **P. Phan**. *The Future of the Asian Churches: The Asian Synod and Ecclesia in Asia*. Quezon City, Philippines: Claretian Publications, 2002; **(F)** *Becoming Local Church*. Quezon City, Philippines: Claretian Publications, 2003; **(G)** "Asia's Dynamic, Missionary Local Churches: FABC Perspectives," *Landas* (Manila) 19:2 (2005): 175-207; **(H)** "FABC Papers Comprehensive Index (2001-2008)," *FABC Papers 125*. Hong Kong: FABC Secretariat, 2008: 1-48; a similar presentation is found in *For All the Peoples of Asia V*. Quezon City, Philippines: Claretian Publications, 2014: Special Appendix; **(I)** *Theology from the Heart of Asia: FABC Doctoral Dissertations I-II*. Quezon City, Philippines: Claretian Publications, 2008; **(J)** "FABC: Asia Needs Renewed Evangelizers," *East Asian Pastoral Review* 50 (2013): 171-188.

LaRousse, W. *Urgency for Mission in the Local Church*. Licentiate Thesis in Missiology, Rome: Pontifical Gregorian University, 1997 [Extensive Bibliography].

Legrand, H. *The Local Church and Catholicity* [*The Jurist* 52 (1992): 1-586]. Washington, DC: The Catholic University of America, 1992.

Malone, E. "Contribution of the Federation of Asian Bishops' Conferences (FABC) to the Evangelizing Mission of the Church in Asia," In *Telling God's Story*. **J. Kroeger** (Ed.)., 127-132. Quezon City, Philippines: Claretian Publications, 2001.

Nocent, A. "The Local Church as Realization of the Church of Christ and Subject of the Eucharist," In *The Reception of Vatican II*. **G. Alberigo** *et al.* (Eds.)., 215-229. Washington, DC: The Catholic University of America Press, 1987.

Phan, P. *Christianity with an Asian Face*. Maryknoll, NY: Orbis Books, 2003.

Pieris, A. "Asia's Non-Semitic Religions and the Mission of

Local Churches," In *An Asian Theology of Liberation*, 35-50. Maryknoll, NY: Orbis Books, 1988.

Quatra, M. *At the Side of the Multitudes: The Kingdom of God and the Mission of the Church in the FABC Documents (1970-1995)*. Quezon City, Philippines: Claretian Publications, 2000.

Quevedo, O. (A) "The Basic Ecclesial Community as a Church Model for Asia," In *A Church on the Threshold*. **M. Seigel** (Ed.)., 193-204. Rome: SEDOS, 1998; **(B)** "Steps Toward Renewing the Church in Asia," *Origins* 29:34 (February 10, 2000): 545, 547-548.

Rosales, G. and **C. Arévalo** (Eds.). *For All the Peoples of Asia I: Federation of Asian Bishops' Conferences Documents from 1970 to 1991*. Maryknoll, NY: Orbis Books and Quezon City, Philippines: Claretian Publications, 1992 and 1997.

Rossignol, R. "Vatican II and Missionary Responsibility of the Particular Churches," *Indian Theological Studies* 17:1 (March, 1980): 34-46.

Tagle, L. "The Renewal that Awaits the Church in Asia," In *It Is the Lord!* 69-92. Manila: Loyola School of Theology, 2003.

Tillard, J. *Church of Churches: The Ecclesiology of Communion* (*Église d'Églises*: 1987). Collegeville, MN: The Liturgical Press, 1992.

Tirimanna, V. (Ed.). *For All the Peoples of Asia V: Federation of Asian Bishops' Conferences Documents from 2007-2012*. Quezon City, Philippines: Claretian Publications, 2014.

Wilfred, F. *et al.* "What the Spirit Says to the Churches (Rev 2:7): A Vademecum on the Pastoral and Theological Orientations of the Federation of Asian Bishops' Conferences (FABC)," *Vidyajyoti* 62:2 (February, 1998): 124-133.

7

NEW EVANGELIZATION TODAY
Key Themes and Asian Links

In Catholic conversation the term "new evangelization" appears frequently these days. Pope Benedict XVI in his message for World Mission Day in October 2011 notes that the Church has the urgent duty to proclaim the Gospel in "new situations" that "require a new evangelization." The pope continues: "This task has not lost its urgency. On the contrary, 'the mission of Christ Redeemer, entrusted to the Church, is still far from being accomplished.... We must commit ourselves with all our energies in its service (RM 1)'." The pope states clearly the scope of the mission of evangelization: "The universal mission involves all, everywhere, and always."

In an apostolic letter dated October 12, 2010, Benedict XVI established a special Vatican agency for the promotion of "new evangelization." This pontifical council has the task of combating the "de-Christianization" of countries that were first evangelized centuries ago. The pope warns of a progressive detachment from religious faith in a wide variety of countries. The new council is to aim at encouraging a clearer understanding of the faith and in helping to "remake the Christian fabric" of human society.

The pope identifies a variety of factors in the weakening of religious faith: advances in science and technology, the widening of individual freedom and lifestyle choices, profound economic changes, the mixing of cultures and ethnic groups brought about by migration, and the growing interdependence among peoples. Such changes have brought about benefits for many people, but they have often been accompanied by "a troubling loss of the sense of the sacred." Undoubtedly, a "new evangelization" is urgently needed. Benedict XVI also determined that the topic for the XIII Ordinary General Assembly of the Synod of Bishops (2012) was to focus on the challenges of the "new evangelization."

This succinct mission catechesis aims at exploring some of the defining traits that characterize the "new evangelization." The topic is extremely broad and rather complex. Thus, this presentation seeks only to describe and present the topic; other discussions are needed to fully analyze the situation and to propose concrete pastoral and mission approaches. To facilitate a clear presentation, this author draws on the writings of several experts (references are found in the brief bibliography). After a discussion of evangelization in general, ten characteristics of the "new evangelization" will be identified; for each trait the author will show its linkages to three pivotal anchors: (a) the Second Vatican Council, (b) recent popes, and (c) the Church in Asia.

Readers will certainly note that the ten defining traits that characterize the new evangelization (selected by this writer) are very similar to important themes discussed during the Second Vatican Council; this is more than a simple coincidence. In fact, this writer finds himself *in full agreement* with a statement by Benedict XVI (September 20, 2012): "We can say that the new evangelization started precisely with the Council, which Blessed John XXIII saw as a new Pentecost...." Indeed, a lengthy discussion on the interconnections would prove most enlightening; yet, for the purposes of this piece, the presentation is admittedly no more than the briefest of introductions to the multifaceted broad topic of "new evangelization."

Exploring Evangelization. The term evangelization is a generally unfamiliar and relatively new concept for many Catholics; only recently has it been gaining wider appreciation. Due to the influence of the Second Vatican Council as well as recent popes, evangelization is now located at the center of the Church's identity and mission—at least theoretically and theologically. These sources and ideas (already mentioned in a previous chapter) have contributed to an understanding of evangelization in all its rich, complex, multi-faceted, and interrelated dimensions. Today, evangelization is necessarily viewed holistically and integrally.

The word "evangelization" is not found in the New Testament; however, *euaggelion* meaning "gospel" or "good news" occurs 72 times, 54 of which are in the Pauline corpus. It has a wide range of meanings: the whole Christian message (Mk 1:1); the good news of Jesus (II Cor 4:4); it is for all (Mk 13:10; 16:15); it is a revelation of God (Gal 1:11-12) which is to be believed (Mk 1:15) and proclaimed (I Cor 9:14, 16, 18). One must risk all for the Gospel (Mk 8:35; Rom 1:16), serve it (Rom 1:1; 15:16), defend it (Phil 1:7, 16). *Euaggelion* is the good news of truth (Gal 2:5, 14), of hope (Col 1:23), of peace (Eph 6:15), of immortality (II Tim 1:10), of the risen Christ (I Cor 15:1ff; II Tim 2:8), and of salvation (Eph 1:13).

Vatican II speaks of mission and evangelization in a variety of contexts: it is especially the bishops' task to promote evangelization by the faithful (CD 6); it is associated with the mission of the laity (AA 2, 6, 20, 26; LG 35); priests are to learn the methods of evangelization (PO 19); the Eucharist is the source and summit of all evangelization (PO 5). The Decree on Missions (AG) is replete with references: "the specific purpose of missionary activity is evangelization and the planting of the Church" (6); "the Church has the obligation and the sacred right to evangelize" (7); catechists have an important task to evangelize (17), as do the laity (21); the call to evangelize arises from a charism of the Spirit (23); various roles are fulfilled by missionary institutes (27), Propaganda Fidei (29), the People of God (35, 36), bishops and priests (38), religious institutes (40), and young Churches (LG 17).

Pope Paul VI (1963-1978), who specifically chose the name Paul to indicate his evangelistic vision for the Church, will always be remembered as a modern missionary pope; he made missionary journeys to all continents; he authored *Evangelii Nuntiandi* (EN), which became the *magna carta* for Catholic evangelization in the last quarter of the second millennium of

Christianity. Without doubt, EN is one of the most important ecclesial documents of the post-Vatican II era. It presents a concise, inspiring, and programmatic challenge for the Church to enthusiastically engage in her God-given mission to preach the Gospel to the contemporary world—to living peoples, with their aspirations and anxieties, their cultures and religions, their hopes and conflicts. Although Paul VI did not use the term "new evangelization," his writings, especially *Evangelii Nuntiandi*, boldly address the topic of evangelization.

Karol Jósef Wojtyla was elected pope on October 16, 1978 and took the name John Paul, clearly identifying himself with the two popes of Vatican II. Under his leadership the papal ministry became focused on evangelization and global mission; he traveled to numerous countries, strengthened local Christian communities, encountered followers of other religions, spoke on the social teachings of the Church, canonized saints and honored blesseds, and met with youth and government leaders. Saint John Paul II asserted that the Second Vatican Council set the direction for his papacy. His eighth encyclical *Redemptoris Missio* (RM) was issued on December 7, 1990; it celebrates the twenty-fifth anniversary of Vatican II's Mission Decree *Ad Gentes* and the fifteenth anniversary of Paul VI's *Evangelii Nuntiandi*. In RM, the pope sounds a clarion call to all Church sectors to renew their commitment to evangelize the world.

John Paul II first mentioned the term "new evangelization" in a speech he gave at Port-au-Prince, Haiti, on March 9, 1983. He declared that the fifth centenary of the beginnings of evangelization of the Americas (1492-1992) should be marked by the beginning of a new era of evangelization, an era which is "new in ardor, methods, and expression." Although the term "new evangelization" was originally used in 1968 by the Latin American bishops meeting at Medellín in their "Message to the Peoples of Latin America," it was John Paul II who gave further clarity and precision to the term through his many speeches, encyclicals, and other documents. Indeed, Saint John Paul II (1978-2005) was enormously effective in promoting evangelization through a wide variety of approaches.

In light of this background from scripture, Vatican II, Paul VI and John Paul II, this presentation, relying on various authors and sources (especially A. Dulles), now turns to a succinct discussion of *ten defining traits* that characterize the new evangelization.

1. Centrality of Christ. The Second Vatican Council sought to link its teachings into the tradition of the Church through *ressourcement* (a return to foundational sources). It employed biblical language and had a clear focus on Christ and the Church. The Council recognized a clear "hierarchy of truths" that placed Christ the Son of God at its highest level (UR 11).

Paul VI spoke clearly of the centrality of Christ: "There can be no true evangelization if the name, the teaching, the life, the promises, the Kingdom and the mystery of Jesus of Nazareth, the Son of God, are not proclaimed" (EN 22). For John Paul II, the proclamation of the mystery of Christ "lies at the heart of the Church's mission and life, as the hinge on which all evangelization turns" (RM 44).

The Church in Asia declares: "To bear witness to Jesus Christ is the supreme service which the Church can offer to the peoples of Asia, for it responds to their profound longing for the Absolute, and it unveils the truths and values which will ensure their integral human development" (*Ecclesia in Asia* 20). The Church in Asia seeks to give credible witness to Christ: "Her one ambition is to continue his mission of service and love, so that all Asians 'may have life and have it abundantly' (Jn 10:10)" (EA 50).

2. Ecumenism. In its document on ecumenism, Vatican II called upon all Christians to bear witness to their common hope (UR 12). The Council also noted that the divisions among Christians are a serious hindrance to the preaching of the Gospel and an authentic witness of life (UR 1).

Paul VI wrote of the importance of the search for Christian

unity; he sought to emphasize "the sign of unity among Christians as the way and instrument of evangelization" (EN 77). In his encyclical *Ut Unum Sint*, John Paul II noted that it is impossible to authentically proclaim the Gospel which speaks of reconciliation, if at the same time, one is not concerned for reconciliation among Christians (UUS 98).

During the Asian Synod (1998), the Synod Fathers "acknowledged that 'the scandal of a divided Christianity is a great obstacle for evangelization in Asia.' In fact, the division among Christians is seen as a counter-witness to Jesus Christ by many in Asia who are searching for harmony and unity through their own religions and cultures" (EA 30). In Asia, "ecumenical dialogue and interreligious dialogue constitute a veritable vocation for the Church" (EA 29).

3. Interreligious Dialogue. The Second Vatican Council issued an entire document on the relationship of the Church with the followers of other faiths (*Nostra Aetate*). "The Catholic Church rejects nothing which is true and holy in these religions.... The Church therefore has this exhortation for her sons and daughters: prudently and lovingly, through dialogue and collaboration with the followers of other religions, and in witness of Christian faith and life, acknowledge, preserve, and promote the spiritual and moral goods found among these people, as well as the values in their society and culture" (NA 2).

Popes Paul VI and John Paul II find no essential conflict between proclamation and authentic interfaith dialogue. Perhaps his greatest affirmation of the importance of dialogue is Pope Paul VI's first encyclical letter *Ecclesiam Suam* (1964) which is heavily devoted to dialogue as a pathway for the Church. One decade later in 1975, he reiterates the Church's profound respect for other religions, but notes that this respect does not imply that the Church would refrain from the proclamation of Jesus Christ (EN 53).

John Paul II devotes three full sections (55-57) of

Redemptoris Missio to exploring relations with the followers of other religions. "Interreligious dialogue is part of the Church's evangelizing mission.... Dialogue is not in opposition to mission *ad gentes*; indeed, it has special links with that mission and is one of its expressions" (RM 55). "Each member of the faithful and all Christian communities are called to practice dialogue" (RM 57).

In Asia, where less than three percent of the population is Christian, the Church actively promotes interfaith dialogue. "Since the Council the Church has consistently shown that she wants to pursue that relationship in a spirit of dialogue.... The dialogue which the Church proposes is grounded in the logic of the Incarnation" (EA 29). "It is therefore important for the Church in Asia to provide suitable models of interreligious dialogue—evangelization in dialogue and dialogue for evangelization—and suitable training for those involved" (EA 31).

4. Religious Freedom. The promotion of new evangelization actually presupposes a full acceptance of the Council document on religious freedom, *Dignitatis Humanae*. The Church asserts that "free exercise of religion in society" is a value "proper to the human spirit" (DH 1). All persons are encouraged to follow their responsible judgment in conscience without external pressure.

Paul VI is eloquent on this topic in *Evangelii Nuntiandi*: "It would certainly be an error to impose something on the consciences of our brethren. But to propose to their consciences the truth of the Gospel and salvation in Jesus Christ, with complete clarity and with total respect for the free options which it presents—'without coercion, or dishonorable or unworthy pressure'—far from being an attack on religious liberty is fully to respect that liberty, which is offered the choice of a way that even non-believers consider noble and uplifting" (EN 80).

Similarly, John Paul II affirms a respectful proclamation of the Gospel. "On her part, the Church addresses people with full respect for their freedom. Her mission does not restrict freedom but rather promotes it. *The Church proposes; she imposes nothing.* She respects individuals and cultures, and she honors the sanctuary of conscience" (RM 39).

The Church in Asia calls upon governments "to recognize religious freedom as a fundamental human right ... [and she invokes the words of Vatican II, noting] the human person has a right to religious freedom. Such freedom consists in this, that all should have such immunity from coercion by individuals, or by social groups, or by any human power, so that no one should be forced to act against his conscience in religious matters, nor prevented from acting according to his conscience, whether in private or in public, whether alone or in association with others, within due limits" (EA 23).

5. Evangelization, a Multi-faceted Process. Vatican II noted: "The split between the faith which many profess and their daily lives deserves to be counted among the more serious errors of our age" (GS 43). Thus, the preaching of the Gospel needs to be tailored to various situations and groups of people. "Indeed, this accommodated preaching of the revealed Word ought to remain the law of all evangelization" (GS 44).

Paul VI constantly promoted a very comprehensive understanding of the evangelization process. He noted: "Any partial and fragmentary definition which attempts to render the reality of evangelization is all its richness, complexity and dynamism does so only at the risk of impoverishing it and even of distorting it" (EN 17). The evangelization process needs constant nuancing, so that it will effectively reach people in the concrete situations of their lives. The call for a "new evangelization" reflects the dynamic and ever-changing challenges the Church's mission encounters.

In the thought of John Paul II one can distinguish three situations of evangelization. There is the "first evangelization" among groups or socio-cultural contexts where Christ and his

Gospel are not known. Next, there is the phase of pastoral care of Christians seeking to live their faith more fully. Finally, there is the situation where people have lost their sense of the faith; "in this case what is needed is a 'new evangelization' or re-evangelization'" (RM 33). Succinctly, the pope affirms that "missionary activity *ad gentes* [is] different from the pastoral care of the faithful, and the new evangelization of the non-practicing" (RM 37).

During the Asian Synod it was affirmed: "The presentation of Jesus Christ as the only Savior needs to follow a *pedagogy* which will introduce people step by step to the full appropriation of the mystery. Clearly, the initial evangelization of non-Christians and the continuing proclamation of Jesus to believers will have to be different in their approach" (EA 20). The participants of Asian Synod stressed "the need to evangelize in a way that appeals to the sensibilities of Asian peoples, and they suggested images of Jesus which would be intelligible to Asian minds and cultures and, at the same time, faithful to Sacred Scripture and Tradition" (EA 20).

6. Social Teaching. Vatican II affirmed that Catholics must always be "attentive to the common good as related to the principles of the moral and social teaching of the Church" (AA 31). Christians are called to involve themselves in temporal affairs, so that "the social order and its development will unceasingly work to the benefit of the human person" (GS 26). The Church's social teaching and involvement spring from the profound realization that "God's Spirit, who with a marvelous providence directs the unfolding of time and renews the face of the earth, is present within these human developments" (GS 26).

Consistent with an integral vision of evangelization, Paul VI affirms that "the Church links human development and salvation in Jesus Christ, but she never identifies [equates] them" (EN 35). "The Church considers it to be undoubtedly important to build up structures which are more human, more just, more respectful of the rights of the person and less oppressive and less enslaving, but she is conscious that the best structures and the most idealized systems soon become inhuman if the inhuman inclinations of the human heart are not made wholesome" (EN 36). Thus, she continually promotes her moral and social teaching.

John Paul II consistently emphasizes Church social teaching and involvement. He notes that there are many places "where action on behalf of integral development and human liberation from all forms of oppression are most urgently needed" (RM 58). The pope affirms: "Authentic human development must be rooted in an ever deeper evangelization" (RM 58). As a force for liberation and development, the Church focuses on the human person, realizing that *"Man is the principal agent of development"* (RM 58).

Church reflection from the Asian context on social involvement is insightful. "The social doctrine of the Church, which proposes a set of principles for reflection, criteria for judgment and directives for action, is addressed in the first place to the members of the Church. It is essential that the faithful engaged in human promotion should have a firm grasp of this precious body of teaching and make it part of their evangelizing mission" (EA 32).

7. Evangelization of Cultures. One entire chapter of the Vatican II document on the Church in the Modern World, *Gaudium et Spes*, is given to the proper development of culture (53-62). The Council notes: "There are many links between the message of salvation and human culture. For God, revealing Himself to His people to the extent of a full manifestation of Himself in His Incarnate Son, has spoken according to the culture proper to different ages.... The Church, sent to all peoples of every time and place..., can enter into communion with various cultural modes, to her own enrichment and theirs too" (GS 58).

Paul VI in his exhortation on evangelization devotes an entire section to the topic of the evangelization of cultures.

He asserts: "What matters is to evangelize human culture and cultures (not in a purely decorative way as it were by applying a thin veneer, but in a vital way, in depth and right to their very roots).... Therefore, every effort must be made to ensure a full evangelization of culture, or more correctly of cultures. They have to be regenerated by an encounter with the Gospel" (EN 20). Probably a penetrating evangelization of cultures stands at the heart of the "new evangelization" project.

In his mission encyclical, John Paul II speaks of various cultural sectors, and he terms them "the modern equivalents of the Areopagus" (RM 37). During the time of Saint Paul, the Areopagus represented the cultural center of the learned people of Athens; "today it can be taken as a symbol of the new sectors in which the Gospel must be proclaimed" (RM 37). In a word, the evangelizing mission of the Church must integrate its message into the "new culture" created by the numerous profound changes in contemporary human society.

Once again, mission reflection from Asia on the topic of culture is replete with helpful insights. "In the process of encountering the world's different cultures, the Church not only transmits her truths and values and renews cultures from within, but she also takes from the various cultures the positive elements already found in them. This is the obligatory path for evangelizers in presenting the Christian faith and in making it part of a people's cultural heritage" (EA 21). This entire process of evangelizing culture and promoting inculturation "has a special urgency today in the multi-ethnic, multi-religious, and multi-cultural situation of Asia, where Christianity is still too often seen as foreign" (EA 21).

8. Social Communication. Avery Cardinal Dulles has asserted that the key traits which are included in the challenge of "new evangelization" and are being presented here have roots in the discussions and documents of the Second Vatican Council. Vatican II in its document on the instruments of social communication, *Inter Mirifica*, notes: "The Catholic Church has been commissioned by the Lord Christ to bring salvation to everyone, and is consequently bound to proclaim the Gospel. Hence, she judges it part of her duty to preach the news of redemption with the aid of the instruments of social communication, and to instruct humanity as well in their worthy use" (IM 3).

With clarity, Paul VI noted the great influence of mass media on the world today. He writes: "Our century is characterized by the mass media or means of social communication, and the first proclamation, catechesis, or the further deepening of the faith cannot do without these means.... When they are put at the service of the Gospel, they are capable of increasing almost indefinitely the area in which the Word of God is heard.... In them she finds a modern and effective version of the pulpit" (EN 45).

In his mission encyclical John Paul II speaks at length about the "world of communication." He asserts: "Since the very evangelization of modern culture depends to a great extent on the influence of the media, it is not enough to use the media simply to spread the Christian message and the Church's authentic teaching. It is also necessary to integrate that message into the 'new culture' created by modern communications. This is a complex issue ... [and it involves] new ways of communicating, with new languages, new techniques, and a new psychology" (RM 37).

The comprehensive vision of evangelization put forth in *Ecclesia in Asia* observes: "Inevitably, the Church's evangelizing mission too is deeply affected by the impact of the mass media.... The exceptional role played by the means of social communication in shaping the world, its cultures and ways of thinking has led to rapid and far-reaching changes in Asian societies.... The Church needs to explore ways of thoroughly integrating the mass media into her pastoral planning and activity, so that by their effective use, the Gospel's power can reach out still further to individuals and entire peoples, and infuse Asian cultures with the values of the Kingdom" (EA 48).

9. Responsibility of All Christians. An older vision of mission and evangelization often saw that mission responsibility was the special concern of priests and sisters, apostolic associations, or various missionary orders of men and women. While these groups remain committed to their founding charism, the Second Vatican Council insisted that "the pilgrim Church is missionary by her very nature" (AG 2) and that "the work of evangelization is a basic duty of the People of God" and everyone must "do their share in missionary work among the nations" (AG 35). In a word, the Church is missionary "from top to bottom," involving everyone—bishops, priests, sisters, laity, and youth.

For Paul VI "it is the whole Church that receives the mission to evangelize, and the work of each individual member is important for the whole" (EN 15). The pope devoted one entire chapter of *Evangelii Nuntiandi* to the "Workers for Evangelization" (59-73). Thus, the commission to spread the Gospel is given to the universal Church (61), the local Churches (62), the pope (67), bishops and priests (68), religious (69), the laity (70), the family (71), and young people (72). One should find in the Church a variety of "diversified ministries" (73)—all at the service of missionary evangelization.

Similar to Paul VI's *Evangelii Nuntiandi*, one finds an entire chapter on "Leaders and Workers in the Missionary Apostolate" in John Paul II's *Redemptoris Missio* (61-76). Several of the same groups noted by Paul VI are mentioned by John Paul II; however, he devotes special sections to "life-long" *ad gentes* missionaries (65-66), diocesan priests (67), contemplatives (69), missionary religious sisters (70), catechists (73), episcopal conferences (76), and the Pontifical Mission Societies (84). Thus, since "all Christians share responsibility for missionary activity," "missionary cooperation" becomes an imperative as diverse communities and individuals share and exercise their "right and duty" of evangelization (RM 77).

Ecclesia in Asia recognizes the multiple and diverse

contributions of missionaries over the centuries. During the "Asian Synod" (1998) the Synod Fathers took advantage of the occasion "to express in a very special way their gratitude to all the missionaries, men and women, religious and lay, foreign and local, who brought the message of Jesus Christ and the gift of faith. A special word of gratitude again must be expressed to all the particular Churches which have sent and still send missionaries to Asia" (EA 20). In the same document, John Paul II noted that the challenge still remains; "I cannot fail to urge the Church in Asia to send forth missionaries, even though she herself needs laborers in the vineyard" (EA 44).

(10) Role of the Holy Spirit. Vatican II and its program of *aggiornamento* bring to the fore the role of the Holy Spirit in the Church, a dimension underemphasized in many earlier presentations of mission. *Ad Gentes*, the Council's Decree on the Church's Missionary Activity, pointed out that the Spirit unceasingly accompanies and guides the Church in her apostolic activities. The Spirit "furnishes the Church with various gifts, both hierarchical and charismatic. He vivifies ecclesiastical institutions as a kind of soul and instills into the hearts of the faithful the same mission spirit which motivated Christ himself" (AG 4). This same Spirit often anticipates the evangelizer's action, opening people's hearts to the Gospel message.

Pope Paul VI is eloquent when presenting the role of the Holy Spirit in missionary activity. "Evangelization will never be possible without the action of the Holy Spirit.... In fact, it is only after the coming of the Holy Spirit on the day of Pentecost that the Apostles depart to all the ends of the earth in order to begin the great work of the Church's evangelization.... Techniques of evangelization are good, but even the most advanced ones could not replace the gentle action of the Spirit.... It must be said that the Holy Spirit is the principal agent of evangelization.... Through the Holy Spirit the Gospel penetrates to the heart of the world" (75).

Saint John Paul II devotes an entire chapter in *Redemptoris*

Missio (21-30) to the pivotal role of the Spirit in evangelization. All mission is "a sending forth in the Spirit" (22). The Spirit gives assurance that evangelizers "will not be alone in this task" (23). From the Spirit the apostle receives "the ability to bear witness to Jesus with 'boldness'" (24). "The Spirit's presence and activity affect not only individuals, but also society and history, peoples, cultures and religions" (28). "Whatever the Spirit brings about in human hearts and in the history of peoples, in cultures and religions, serves as a preparation for the Gospel" (29). Again, John Paul II reiterates that the Spirit is "the principal agent of mission" (30).

In the multi-cultural and pluri-religious Asian context, the action of the Spirit is paramount. "The Spirit gathers into unity all kinds of people, with their different customs, resources, and talents, making the Church a sign of the communion of all humanity.... [Thus] the Holy Spirit is the prime agent of evangelization" (EA 17). The Church looks to the Holy Spirit to continue to prepare the peoples of Asia for the saving dialogue with the Savior of all.... Committed to being a genuine sign and instrument of the Spirit's action in the complex realities of Asia..., the Church ceaselessly cries out: Come, Holy Spirit! Fill the hearts of your faithful and enkindle in them the fire of your love" (EA 18).

Conclusion. This presentation of ten defining traits that characterize the "new evangelization" may appear to readers to be overwhelming. Yes, the task of evangelization in the contemporary world is genuinely complex and awesomely challenging. Indeed, no individual can hope to accomplish any more than a small fragment of the total task. Thus, it is imperative that all segments of the Church collaborate in this beautiful endeavor, believing that, as John Paul II affirmed, "God is preparing a great springtime for Christianity.... Christian hope sustains us in committing ourselves fully to the new evangelization and to worldwide mission" (RM 86).

In 1975 Paul VI issued two interrelated apostolic exhortations: *Evangelii Nuntiandi* (Evangelization in the

Modern World) and *Gaudete in Domino* (On Christian Joy). The pope constantly asserted that if the Gospel is not heard from "joyful evangelizers," it will not be heard at all by contemporary humanity. The lack of joy and hope is an obstacle to effective evangelization. Paul VI believed that joy would enable the world of our time "to receive the Good News not from evangelizers who are dejected, discouraged, impatient or anxious, but from ministers of the Gospel whose lives glow with fervor, who have first received the joy of Christ, and who are willing to risk their lives so that the Kingdom may be proclaimed and the Church established in the midst of the world" (EN 80).

The success of the "new evangelization" requires "renewed evangelizers." Jesuit Pierre Teilhard de Chardin wrote: "Joy is the most infallible sign of the presence of God." Joy is convincing; joy evangelizes. All the complex dimensions of the "new evangelization" will not overwhelm those whose lives have been transformed by a joyful encounter with the Risen Lord. We must listen frequently to the admonition of Saint Paul: "Rejoice in the Lord always. I shall say it again: rejoice! Your kindness should be known to all. The Lord is near" (Gal 4:4). Be transformed by joy. Become a herald of the new evangelization! Surrender to the "Lord of Joy" for he is: *Jesu, Joy of Man's Desiring*!

COMMON ABBREVIATIONS

AA	*Apostolicam Actuositatem*	Laity
AG	*Ad Gentes*	Missionary Activity
CD	*Christus Dominus*	Bishops
DH	*Dignitatis Humanae*	Religious Freedom
DV	*Dei Verbum*	Divine Revelation
EA	*Ecclesia in Asia*	Church in Asia (John Paul II)
EN	*Evangelii Nuntiandi*	Evangelization Today (Paul VI)
GD	*Gaudete in Domino*	On Christian Joy (Paul VI)

GS	*Gaudium et Spes*	Church Today
IM	*Inter Mirifica*	Social Communications
LG	*Lumen Gentium*	Church
NA	*Nostra Aetate*	Non-Christian Religions
PO	*Presbyterorum Ordinis*	Priests
RM	*Redemptoris Missio*	Mission of the Redeemer (John Paul II)
SC	*Sacrosanctum Concilium*	Sacred Liturgy
UR	*Unitatis Redintegratio*	Ecumenism
UUS	*Ut Unum Sint*	That All Be One (John Paul II)

THE NEW EVANGELIZATION
A Selected Bibliography

Alappat, V. "New Evangelization: Challenge from Pauline Perspective," *Bible Bhashyam* 39:2 (2013): 116-128.

Barron, R. **(A)** *Catholicism: The New Evangelization* (text and video) [in collaboration with Brandon Vogt]. Skokie, IL: Word on Fire Catholic Ministries, 2013; **(B)** "To Evangelize the Culture," *Chicago Studies* 52:1 (Spring, 2013): 7-27.

Benedict XVI. **(A)** "Pontifical Council for Promoting New Evangelization Established," *Origins* 40:25 (November 25, 2010): 394-396; **(B)** "Popular Piety and the New Evangelization," *L'Osservatore Romano* (English Edition), 44:15 (April 13, 2011): 4; **(C)** "Address to Pontifical Council for Promoting New Evangelization," *Origins* 41:6 (June 16, 2011): 90-91; **(D)** "World Mission Sunday 2011 Message," See: www.vatican. va.; **(E)** "The New Evangelization started with Vatican II," *L'Osservatore Romano* (English Edition), 45:39 (September 26, 2012): 5; **(F)** "Missionaries of the New Evangelization" [Message for 2013 World Youth Day], *L'Osservatore Romano* (English Edition), 45:47 (November 21, 2012): 12-14; **(G)** "Ecumenism in the Time of the New Evangelization," *L'Osservatore Romano* (English Edition), 45:47 (November 21, 2012): 7-8.

Boguslawski, S. and **R. Martin** (Eds.). *The New Evangelization: Overcoming the Obstacles*. New York: Paulist Press, 2008.

Boucher, J. and **T. Boucher.** *Sharing the Faith that You Love: Four Simple Ways to be Part of the New Evangelization.* Frederick, MD: The Word among Us Press, 2014.

Boyack, K. "What Is 'New' in the New Evangelization?" *The Living Light* 30:1 (1993): 3-8.

Canilang, S. *The New Evangelization: The Development of the Concept and Its Comprehensive Meaning* (ICLA Monographs 15). Quezon City, Philippines: Institute for Consecrated Life in Asia (ICLA), 2013.

Catholic Bishops Conference of the Philippines (CBCP). "Live Christ, Share Christ" [Pastoral Letter on the Era of New Evangelization], *CBCP Monitor* 16:15 (July 16-29, 2012): B-1.

Champagne, C. "New Evangelization: New Challenges for the Church's Mission," *Origins* 37:22 (November 8, 2007): 341-347.

Clark, E. "What Is New about the New Evangelization?" *Origins* 36:1 (May 18, 2006): 1-7.

Clark, F. "Asian Saints and Blesseds, and the New Evangelization," *Studia Missionalia* 48 (1999): 313-325.

Dulles, A. (A) "John Paul II and the New Evangelization," *America* 166:3 (February 1, 1992): 52-59, 69-72; (B) "John Paul II and the New Evangelization," *Studia Missionalia* 48 (1999): 165-180; (C) *Evangelization for the Third Millennium*. New York: Paulist Press, 2009.

Fisichella, R. (A) *The New Evangelization: Responding to the Challenge of Indifference.* Balwyn, Australia: Freedom

Publishing, 2012; **(B)** "Jesus and the Year of Faith: Impelling the New Evangelization," *Origins* 42:14 (September 6, 2012): 217-221.

Franciscus (Pope Francis). *Evangelii Gaudium (The Joy of the Gospel).* Rome: Vatican Press, 2013.

Hahn, S. "Mass Evangelization," *America* 208:13 (April 22, 2013): 13-17.

Hater, R. *The Parish Guide to the New Evangelization: An Action Plan for Sharing the Faith.* Huntington, IN: Our Sunday Visitor, Inc., 2013.

John Paul II. "Needed: A New Evangelization," *Origins* 20:2 (May 24, 1990): 27-30.

Kroeger, J. (A) *The Future of the Asian Churches: The Asian Synod and Ecclesia in Asia* (Edited with **P. Phan**). Quezon City, Philippines: Claretian Publications, 2002; **(B)** "A Church Living to Evangelize: Recent Popes and Integral Evangelization," in: *Becoming Local Church: Historical, Theological and Missiological Essays.* 55-86. Quezon City, Philippines: Claretian Publications; 2003; **(C)** *Exploring the Treasures of Vatican II.* Quezon City, Philippines: Claretian Publications and Jesuit Communications, 2011; **(D)** *A Vatican II Journey: Fifty Milestones.* Makati City, Philippines: ST PAULS, 2012; **(E)** *The Gift of Mission: Yesterday, Today, Tomorrow.* Maryknoll, NY: Orbis Books, 2013.

Levada, W. "Giving Reasons for Our Hope: A New Apologetics for the New Evangelization," *Origins* 43:3 (May 23, 2013): 33-42.

Malone, P. "Media and Mission: New Ways of Evangelization," *Catholic International* 12:4 (November 2001): 81-84.

Martin, R. (A) *John Paul II and the New Evangelization*

(Edited with **P. Williamson**). Cincinnati, OH: Servant Books, 2006; **(B)** *The Urgency of the New Evangelization: Answering the Call*. Huntington, IN: Our Sunday Visitor, Inc., 2013.

Nodar, D. "What Are Characteristics of the New Evangelization?" *See*: www.christlife.org/resources

Ouellet, M. "The New Evangelization and the Mass Media," *Origins* 38:6 (June 19, 2008): 93-98.

Pable, M. "A New Language for the New Evangelization?" *The Priest* 69:2 (February 2013): 45-47, 49, 51.

Pattaparambil, A. (Ed.). *New Evangelization and Migration: Transforming Perspecives*. Bangalore, India: Asian Trading Corporation, 2012.

Pushparajan, A. **(A)** "The 'New Evangelization' in the Asian Context of Interreligious Dialogue:" I-II," *Vidyajyoti* 76: 4-5 (April-May, 2012): 298-306, 371-379; **(B)** "Dialogue with Non-Believers and the 'New Evangelization'," *Vidyajyoti* 76:9 (September, 2012): 664-680.

Routhier, G. "Vatican II as the Point of Departure for the New Evangelization," *Doctrine and Life* 62:3 (March 2012): 21-39.

Rymarz, R. **(A)** "Conversion and the New Evangelization: A Perspective from Lonergan," *The Heythrop Journal* 51:5 (2010): 753-767; **(B)** "John Paul II and the 'New Evangelization': Origins and Meaning." *See*: www.aejt.com.au

Stringer, B. "The New Evangelisation," *The Pastoral Review* 8:1 (2012): 37-42.

Sullivan, J. *Opening the Door of Faith: A Study Guide for Catechetics and the New Evangelization*. Huntington, IN: Our Sunday Visitor, Inc., 2012.

Synod of Bishops. **(A)** "The New Evangelization for the Transmission of the Christian Faith" (Lineamenta for 2012 Synod of Bishops). *See*: www.vatican.va; **(B)** "Final Message: XIII Ordinary General Assembly (2012). *See*: www.vatican.va.

Thomas, J. and **V. Sagayam** (Eds.). *New Evangelization: Asian Perspectives.* Pune, India: Ishvani Kendra and Bandra, Bombay, India: St Pauls, 2012.

United States Conference of Catholic Bishops. *Disciples Called to Witness: The New Evangelization.* Washington, DC: USCCB, 2012; also in: *Origins* 42:5 (June 7, 2012): 69-79.

Wang, S. *The New Evangelisation: What it Is and How to do It.* London: Catholic Truth Society, 2013.

Witherup, R. *Saint Paul and the New Evangelization.* Collegeville, MN: Liturgical Press, 2013.

Wuerl, D. **(A)** "Pastoral Letter on the New Evangelization," *Origins* 40:16 (September 23, 2010): 241-251; **(B)** "What is the Synod on the New Evangelization?" *The Priest* 68:10 (October 2012): 10-13; **(C)** *New Evangelization: Passing on the Catholic Faith Today.* Huntington, IN: Our Sunday Visitor, Inc., 2013.

BIOGRAPHICAL DATA

Father James H. Kroeger, a Maryknoll Missioner, born in Wisconsin, USA on December 4, 1945, was ordained a priest on May 17, 1975. He has served mission in Asia (Philippines and Bangladesh) since his 1970 arrival in the Orient, working in parishes and serving mostly in the education-formation apostolate of seminarians, catechists, and lay leaders.

Father Kroeger has two Masters Degrees in Pastoral and Systematic Theology. He holds both licentiate and doctorate degrees in Missiology (Mission Theology) from the Gregorian University in Rome. His doctoral dissertation (1985) bears the popular title: *The Philippine Church and Evangelization*.

Currently he teaches systematic theology, missiology, and Islamics at the Loyola School of Theology (Ateneo de Manila); he is also a regular professor at the East Asian Pastoral Institute and at the Mother of Life Catechetical Center. He is the President of the Philippine Association of Catholic Missiologists (PACM), Mission Consultant for the Federation of Asian Bishops' Conferences (FABC) Office of Evangelization, Secretary-Convener of FABC: AMSAL (FABC: Asian-born Missionary Societies of Apostolic Life Forum), and a member of the Philippine Catholic Mission Council established by the Catholic Bishops' Conference of the Philippines (CBCP) Commission on Mission. Kroeger is fluent in the Cebuano and Tagalog languages of the Philippines.

He has produced numerous theological-catechetical books (see separate list). He is a regular contributor of journal articles to such periodicals as: *SEDOS Bulletin*, *Studia Missionalia*, *Verbum SVD*, *Vidyajyoti*, *East Asian Pastoral Review*, *FABC Papers*, *African Ecclesial Review*, *Review for Religious*, *World Mission* (Manila), *Third Millennium*, *Mission Today*, and *Landas: Journal of Loyola School of Theology* (Manila). Since 1986, Kroeger continues to serve as the Asian representative on the editorial advisory board of Orbis Books of Maryknoll, New York. From 1990-1996, Kroeger was the Asia-Pacific Assistant on the Maryknoll General Council. He may be contacted at: jhkroeger@gmail.com or Maryknoll Box 285; Greenhills Post Office; 1502 Metro Manila, Philippines.

BOOKS BY JAMES H. KROEGER *

WALKING IN THE LIGHT OF FAITH.
  Makati City, Philippines: ST PAULS, 2014.

THE GIFT OF MISSION: YESTERDAY, TODAY, TOMORROW.
  Maryknoll, New York: Orbis Books, 2013.
    Published in "e-book" format, 2013.

A VATICAN II JOURNEY: FIFTY MILESTONES.
  Philippine Edition: Makati City, Philippines:
    ST PAULS, 2012, 2013.
  Bahasa-Indonesia Edition: 50 Jejak Konsili Vatikan II.
    Yogyakarta, Indonesia: Penerbit Kanisius, 2013.
  Chinese-English Bilingual Edition: Taipei: Kuangchi
    Cultural Group, 2013.

EXPLORING THE TREASURES OF VATICAN II.
  Quezon City, Philippines: Claretian Publications and
    Jesuit Communications, 2011.

THE DOCUMENTS OF VATICAN COUNCIL II.
  Pasay City, Philippines: Paulines, 2011.

A FIERY FLAME: ENCOUNTERING GOD'S WORD.
  Quezon City, Philippines: Claretian Publications,
    Insta Publications, and Jesuit Communications, 2010.

JESUS: A PORTRAIT (Philippine Edition)
  Quezon City, Philippines: Claretian Publications
    and Jesuit Communications, 2010.

* NOTE: This list includes books produced by James Kroeger as
author/editor, either alone or in collaboration with others.

MIGRATION: OPENING PATHWAYS OF THE CHURCH'S MISSION.
Quezon City, Philippines: Scalabrini Migration Center, 2010.

DIALOGUE: INTERPRETIVE KEY FOR THE
LIFE OF THE CHURCH IN ASIA.
Hong Kong: Federation of Asian Bishops' Conferences, 2010.

THEOLOGY FROM THE HEART OF ASIA: I - II.
Quezon City, Philippines: Claretian Publications, 2008.

ARE NOT OUR HEARTS BURNING? 75 YEARS OF THE
PONTIFICAL MISSION SOCIETIES OF THE PHILIPPINES.
Sampaloc, Manila: Pontifical Mission Societies, 2008.

FABC PAPERS PERIODIC INDEX: Papers 101-125 (2001-2008).
Hong Kong: Federation of Asian Bishops' Conferences, 2008.

ONCE UPON A TIME IN ASIA:
STORIES OF HARMONY AND PEACE.
North American Edition: Maryknoll, New York:
Orbis Books, 2006.
Published in "e-book" format, 2013.
Asian Edition: Quezon City, Philippines: Claretian
Publications and Jesuit Communications, 2006.
Polish Edition: *Pewnego Razu w Azji*. Kraków:
Wydawnictwo WAM, 2007.
Vietnamese Edition: Vietnamese Institute of
Philosophy and Religion, 2008.
Thai Edition: Bangkok: Catholic Social
Communications of Thailand, 2008.
Italian Edition: Armonie: Volti dell'Asia, Volti di Dio.
Bologna: EMI, 2008.
Chinese-English Bilingual Edition: Taipei: Kuangchi
Cultural Group, 2008.
Bahasa-Indonesia Edition: Kisah-kisah Harmoni dan Damai.
Yogyakarta, Indonesia: Penerbit Kanisius, 2008.
Bengali Edition: Dhaka, Bangladesh: Holy Spirit
Major Seminary, 2010.
Korean Edition: Seoul, Korea, 2014.

THE SECOND VATICAN COUNCIL AND THE CHURCH IN ASIA:
READINGS AND REFLECTIONS.
Hong Kong: Federation of Asian Bishops' Conferences, 2006.

INCULTURATION IN ASIA: DIRECTIONS,
INITIATIVES, AND OPTIONS.
Hong Kong: Federation of Asian Bishops' Conferences, 2005.

THE CHALLENGE OF RELIGIOUS DIVERSITY IN MIGRATION.
Quezon City, Philippines: Scalabrini Migration Center, 2005.

BECOMING LOCAL CHURCH: HISTORICAL,
THEOLOGICAL AND MISSIOLOGICAL ESSAYS.
Quezon City, Philippines: Claretian Publications, 2003.

LOCAL CHURCH, DIALOGUE AND CONVERSION.
Hong Kong: Federation of Asian Bishops' Conferences, 2003.

SUGINLI ANG KALIBUTAN: CEBUANO TRANSLATION OF:
TELL THE WORLD: CATECHETICAL MODULES FOR
MISSION ANIMATION.
Cebu City, Philippines: Archdiocesan Commission on
Mission, 2003.

THE FUTURE OF THE ASIAN CHURCHES:
THE ASIAN SYNOD AND *ECCLESIA IN ASIA*.
Quezon City, Philippines: Claretian Publications, 2002.

SONS OF SAN JOSE: THE JOSEFINO SPIRIT—A PROFILE.
Quezon City, Philippines: San Jose Seminary Alumni
Association, 2002.

TELLING GOD'S STORY: NATIONAL MISSION CONGRESS 2000.
Quezon City, Philippines: Claretian Publications, 2001.

FABC PAPERS COMPREHENSIVE INDEX: 1976-2001.
Hong Kong: Federation of Asian Bishops' Conferences, 2001.

TELL THE WORLD: CATECHETICAL MODULES FOR
MISSION ANIMATION.
Quezon City, Philippines: Claretian Publications, 2000.

ECCLESIA IN ASIA: COMMENTARIES.
Shillong, India: Mission Today Editions, 2000.

MISSION ANIMATION RESOURCE KIT (MARK).
Manila, Philippines: Catholic Bishops' Conference
of the Philippines, 2000.

ASIA-CHURCH IN MISSION.
Quezon City, Philippines: Claretian Publications, 1999.

LIVING MISSION IN ASIA.
Hong Kong: Federation of Asian Bishops' Conferences, 1999.

REMEMBERING OUR BISHOP JOSEPH W. REGAN, M.M.
Quezon City, Philippines: Claretian Publications, 1998.

CONTEMPORARY MISSION ISSUES.
A Series of eleven pamphlets on Mission Issues.
Maryknoll, New York: Maryknoll Press, 1995-1997.

LIVING MISSION: CHALLENGES IN EVANGELIZATION TODAY.
North American Edition: Maryknoll, New York:
Orbis Books, 1994, 2009.
Asian Edition: Quezon City, Philippines: Claretian
Publications, 1994.

MISSION TODAY: CONTEMPORARY THEMES IN MISSIOLOGY.
Hong Kong: Federation of Asian Bishops' Conferences, 1991.

INTERRELIGIOUS DIALOGUE: CATHOLIC PERSPECTIVES.
Davao City, Philippines: Mission Studies Institute, 1990.

KNOWING CHRIST JESUS: A CHRISTOLOGICAL SOURCEBOOK.
Quezon City, Philippines: Claretian Publications, 1989.

CHURCH TRULY ALIVE: JOURNEY TO THE
FILIPINO REVOLUTION.
Davao City, Philippines: Mission Studies Institute, 1988.

ADVANCED CEBUANO COLLOQUIAL EXPRESSIONS.
Davao City, Philippines: Institute of Language and
Culture, 1986.

THE PHILIPPINE CHURCH AND
EVANGELIZATION: 1965-1984.
Rome, Italy: Gregorian University Press, 1985.